WORKFUEL

THE PRODUCTIVITY NINJA GUIDE TO NUTRITION

BOOST PERFORMANCE	IMPROVE FOCUS	EAT YOUR WAY TO SUCCESS

GRAHAM ALLCOTT & COLETTE HENEGHAN

ICON

Published in the UK and USA in 2019
by Icon Books Ltd, Omnibus Business Centre,
39–41 North Road, London N7 9DP
email: info@iconbooks.com
www.iconbooks.com

Sold in the UK, Europe and Asia
by Faber & Faber Ltd, Bloomsbury House,
74–77 Great Russell Street,
London WC1B 3DA or their agents

Distributed in the UK, Europe and Asia
by Grantham Book Services,
Trent Road, Grantham NG31 7XQ

Distributed in Australia and New Zealand
by Allen & Unwin Pty Ltd, PO Box 8500,
83 Alexander Street, Crows Nest, NSW 2065

Distributed in South Africa
by Jonathan Ball,
Office B4, The District,
41 Sir Lowry Road, Woodstock 7925

Distributed in India
by Penguin Books India,
7th Floor, Infinity Tower – C, DLF Cyber City,
Gurgaon 122002, Haryana

Distributed in the USA
by Publishers Group West,
1700 Fourth Street, Berkeley, CA 94710

Distributed in Canada
by Publishers Group Canada,
76 Stafford Street, Unit 300,
Toronto, Ontario M6J 2S1

ISBN: 978-178578-459-0

The contents of this book are based on the best information available to the authors at the time of writing. Neither the authors nor the publisher is engaged in providing any medical diagnosis or treatment to individual readers, and the book does not constitute medical advice. If you have any specific questions about any medical matter always consult a doctor or appropriate professional. Neither the authors nor the publisher shall be liable or responsible for any loss, injury or damage allegedly arising from any information or suggestion in this book.

Typeset by Marie Doherty

Printed and bound in Great Britain
by Clays Ltd, Elcograf S.p.A.

ABOUT THE AUTHORS

GRAHAM ALLCOTT

Graham Allcott is a speaker, an entrepreneur and the founder of Think Productive, one of the world's leading providers of business productivity workshops and coaching. Think Productive's client list includes eBay, the Bill & Melinda Gates Foundation, Heineken and GlaxoSmithKline.

Think Productive workshops include:

> How to be a Productivity Ninja
> Getting Your Inbox to Zero
> Email Etiquette
> Fixing Meetings

Graham is the author of the international bestseller *How to be a Productivity Ninja*, as well as *A Practical Guide to Productivity* and *How to be a Study Ninja*. He is also host of the popular business podcast *Beyond Busy*.

Prior to founding Think Productive, Graham held various roles, including co-founder of Intervol, chief executive of Student Volunteering England and adviser to the UK government on youth and community issues.

Despite an intolerance of failure elsewhere in his life, he is an Aston Villa season ticket holder and an avid follower of the Toronto Blue Jays baseball team.

Graham lives in Brighton, UK.

COLETTE HENEGHAN

Colette Heneghan is a speaker, a coach and founder of Optimum Living, a well-being organization that has designed, managed and delivered successful high-impact health and well-being programmes across the world. Optimum Living's client list ranges from large multinational corporates such as Vodafone and BT to small charities and professional sports teams.

Colette delivers workshops covering topics such as nutrition for energy, thriving leadership, understanding and managing stress and the power of sleep.

Prior to founding Optimum Living, Colette worked in the global corporate world for over ten years. She has an MSc in personalized nutrition, a BSc in business information technology and diplomas in herbal medicine and naturopathic nutrition.

Colette is a foodie, an aspiring yogi, entrepreneur and eternal student. She grew up in Manchester, where even as a child she was passionate about food, plants and natural approaches to health. A passion that extended to practical application on unsuspecting friends – thankfully Anna, Peter and Philip all lived to tell the tale!

Colette lives in London, UK.

CONTENTS

INTRODUCTION

INTRODUCTION FROM GRAHAM ALLCOTT

Welcome to *Work Fuel*. We're so excited to be bringing you this book, which is the result of a few years of collaboration between Colette and myself. Colette has been an inspiration as well as a fountain of knowledge on the topics of nutrition and well-being, and on developing the habits and strategies for peak performance. I'm honoured to be working with her to bring you the first of our series of Productivity Ninja Guides.

Since the release of *How to be a Productivity Ninja*, I've spent the last few years spreading the Ninja gospel around the world. If you're here because you're already a convert to the way of the Productivity Ninja, then thank you. But if you don't know what the heck I'm talking about, then allow me to briefly explain.

A Productivity Ninja is someone who takes control of their own productivity, with great systems and clear thinking that cuts through all the information overload and inefficiency that seem to plague our working lives. There are nine characteristics of the Productivity Ninja, which are:

> **Zen-like calm**: Having a singular, 'in-the-present-moment' focus for your work, by getting all the myriad of ideas, nags and tasks out of your head and into a 'second brain' (a series of lists that help you manage everything you're working on).

Ruthlessness: Learning the powerful art of saying no to anything that gets in the way – whether that be your own distractions or other people's priorities.

Weapon-savvy: Using apps/tools to optimize productivity.

Stealth and camouflage: Making yourself deliberately less available, so that you can get some work done, away from the noisy world of the internet or the open-plan office.

Unorthodoxy: Questioning the rules and the status quo, and caring less about how you get there than about reaching the goal.

Agility: Being nimble and able to react to changing circumstances.

Mindfulness: Taking a mindful approach to work, whether that's recognizing the importance of meditation and other mindfulness tools, or whether it's approaching your to-do list or meetings mindfully so that you're aware of your own emotions or resistance.

Preparedness: Adopting a mentality of preparing and thinking ahead, so that you're organized and ready for whatever comes your way.

Human, not superhero: Productivity Ninjas may often look like superheroes, because so much seems to go to plan. But what's worth remembering is that we're all human. There are no special powers or shortcuts to success and we all get things wrong sometimes (so go easy on yourself – and others!).

I've lived and worked under the Ninja philosophy for many years now (after spending the first years of my career as a self-confessed disorganized mess), but I'm still human, not superhero.

A couple of years ago, I was finding that while I was sticking to these Ninja characteristics, I was still experiencing periods of very low energy and hence poor productivity. I would often experience low moods, especially in the afternoons, and it got to the point where I realized I needed help. I'd met Colette a couple of times before, so I asked her to become my nutrition coach. I didn't really know what kind of results I could expect, but I knew that food and fuel are vital for the brain's performance. However, the level of additional energy I managed to find was shocking – and I didn't think I was eating *that* badly before.

The changes for me are permanent and habitual. I probably don't spend any more time cooking or preparing food than I ever did. Many of the nutrient-rich meals I'm making are simple and fast to prepare. What's changed is I now have more of a strategy to make sure the meals I'm serving myself are serving my brain's functions, too. I'd previously experienced a lot of very low-energy days where I didn't feel like working at all, and most days I'd feel an energy dip after lunch. Now all that's gone. I've more or less cut out caffeine and don't feel as sluggish when I wake up. When things get busy or I've got a lot on, I feel like I can absorb stress like a sponge – much like I did in the first few years of my career – but this time I'm helping myself rest and recover, to keep things sustainable too. And while vanity wasn't part of the motivation for working with Colette, for the first time in my life, friends who I haven't seen for a while say things like 'You're looking well', or 'Have you lost weight?', which, to be honest, still feels weird!

For a few months, we had a daily WhatsApp chat, where I would post pictures of every meal and Colette would comment: 'doing great, but add some more protein in there', 'switch this for that. Simple change', and occasionally '… Oh dear. [Sad face]'. What this process taught me – aside from a huge wealth of little snippets of useful nutritional information, was that at times we all need a push to think about what we're eating. Colette would challenge my occasional 'I'm too busy for this' narrative and remind me that her own work schedule was as busy as mine (as she sent me back a picture of a salad that had been thrown together from brilliant ingredients).

'You eat well when you have good ingredients in your fridge', I remember her messaging me. Ah. I get this now. Ninja prepared-ness! I wrote about this in *How to be a Productivity Ninja*. A lot of it wasn't actually about food, but about gently coaching my resistance against changes in habit.

In fact, there are so many crossovers and similarities in the way Colette thinks about food and the way I think about productivity and work, *Work Fuel* began to feel like an obvious joint creation for us to put our well-fuelled minds to. And here we are.

This is the nutrition plan for people who can't usually be arsed with nutrition. It's a busy person's guide to eating well. The Work Fuel Way is a lifestyle that will support healthier and better choices at work, but it will also give you more energy, better health and less stress in the rest of your life, too.

So, if you're not lucky enough to work for a company that's running workshops in this kind of stuff, or in a position to hire your own personal nutrition coach, here's all the wisdom from two workshop leaders, a master's-level qualified nutritionist and coach (Colette, obviously) and one extremely willing nutritional guinea pig (me), for the price of a takeaway.

INTRODUCTION FROM COLETTE HENEGHAN

If you want your brain and body to perform at their best, they have to be fed the right kind of fuel. Every meal counts. All the food we eat is either potential brain fuel or potential brain fog.

In my first career in global sales and management, my daily food choices were an afterthought. I would just grab food when I could, and regularly swapped eating time for catching up and meetings. It seemed like there was never enough time to fit in all the meetings, calls and emails in my day. My lunch breaks were few and far between. I survived some days on tea and biscuits provided in client meetings. At least it was some food, and surely skipping meals was a good thing as it meant fewer calories … right?

The challenge wasn't the role itself; instead it was my energy levels and an inability to concentrate on any one thing for too long. I never made the connection that my poor concentration was because I hadn't had breakfast, or that if I had eaten, it was likely to have been a sugary, so-called 'healthy', cereal. My lunch choices were not gearing me up for proactive attention in the afternoon. In fact, I was usually feeling more like I wanted a nap (a problem exacerbated by dark meeting rooms and endless slides – a colleague and I would literally stab each other with a pen whenever we looked like we might nod off).

As it turned out, I wasn't alone.

When I mentioned this to my colleagues, they said that they were tired too and often struggled with their concentration and energy levels. They said things like 'this is the reality of working life, just get used to it!' After all, we were all still delivering our numbers, closing business, managing our clients and getting results. So, what was the problem?

The thing is, health is so much more than not being off sick.

True health is a state of high performance: having the energy, vibrancy and vitality to do whatever you want to do. I may have been delivering on the numbers, but was I missing out in other areas of life? The answer is most certainly yes.

I was on so many professional courses in my corporate career, from time management to negotiation skills, networking to presenting with impact. Not one of these mentioned that in order to deliver in all of these areas to the best of my ability, I had to be properly fuelled.

Following some personal research and a desire to make some changes, I made a few simple upgrades to my food choices and cut out some of the more obvious energy zappers and almost immediately saw improvements in my performance at work and in my mood. I simply got more stuff done. It sparked a real passion to learn more of the science behind it, so I resigned from my job and went back to uni. I spent five years in full-time study, completing a range of courses, another undergraduate qualification and a master's in nutritional science.

Funnily enough, I have subsequently managed to create a role that is just as busy and demanding as my first career. My working week as a performance and nutrition coach is still filled with business travel, meetings, conference calls, webinars and conferences. Yet the difference in my energy, productivity and vitality is light years away and I will not compromise on these benefits ever again.

Despite all the information out there, we are still not doing a lot of the basics when it comes to food. Why? Because knowledge alone rarely stimulates behavioural change, plus our behaviour often strays from our good intentions. We need to make food decisions many times a day and we just can't devote too much of our limited, precious decision-making capacity to each choice, so our eating tends to be habit driven (like most of our lives).

The importance of developing the right habits should not be under-estimated; that's why each chapter in this book has a call to action, with some bite-sized upgrades you can make, and why there is a whole chapter about making it stick. Creating stickiness is where the magic happens and where long-lasting change begins. The only imperative is that you have to start – and it's a good idea to start small; you'll learn why.

Let's begin by giving more focus to what is on our daily menu, rather than our daily agenda, by loading our forks with real food that is literally going to feed our productivity, performance and health. What are you waiting for? Welcome to *Work Fuel*!

1.
THE WORK FUEL WAY

They say that time is our most precious resource. It's not. Our most precious resource is our attention. And the most precious resource of all is what we call 'proactive attention' –

'The best investment you can make is in yourself.'
– Warren Buffett

the two or three hours each day when we're fully alert, our energy is high, and we feel like we can take on the world. Spending your proactive attention wisely is one of the most important ways to be a Productivity Ninja. Attention management is about how to make the most out of a finite resource.

But what if there was also a way to *increase* proactive attention? To actually have more of it? To feel in your peak state for longer during every working day, and to spend less time sitting unproductively at your desk feeling frazzled. That would truly feel like magically getting more hours in the day! We're here to show you how.

There are a million food books out there and hundreds of business productivity books too, but this book, which combines our years of experience coaching individuals and teams at work on their food (Colette) and their productivity (Graham), is the bridge between the two. It's a book backed up by hard scientific fact, not trendy fad diet plans. Our philosophy is that starting with practical reality is better than presenting unobtainable perfection. No 30-minute meals that take two hours to make, no soft-focus pretty pictures of perfect kitchens and Instagram lifestyle crap. This is a food book for busy people, who care about what they eat, but are too busy to get it right all the time. This is what you really need to know about the relationship between potatoes and peak performance. Between peaches and productivity. Between paella and … you get the idea. Let's get started.

HOW TO USE THIS BOOK

In this chapter we'll introduce you to the nine essentials of the Work Fuel Way. These are the key principles, habits and attitudes that will give you a rocket boost for the mind, body and soul. The Work Fuel Way is a mindset – a new way to think about how you approach your food and the creation of energy to nourish your body, soul, work and life. In Chapter 2, we'll look specifically at the science of food and cognition: which foods bring us the best energy? What should we avoid? Some of this will feel like common sense but we think some of it will shock you, too.

Once we have this foundation, the next three chapters will walk through common pitfalls and tactics for getting the best out of each of the three meals of the day. These chapters will provide the detail of what foods to eat at certain times of the day, how to prep it, how to make it easy and how to make it happen.

Chapter 6, 'Being Label-savvy', will explain how you can become a food label detective, so that you can start to pick food items up, scan them with your eyes, and make an informed choice as to whether to include them in your meal, or leave them behind.

Chapter 7 will discuss 'Thriving on the Go', with ideas of what to do when you are at the mercy of predetermined food choices, how you can mitigate them, and some useful work-arounds.

Chapter 8, 'How to Shop', will focus on how we can be much more Ninja prepared in the supermarket and the kitchen, and on learning to shop in the most ruthless way.

Chapter 9 is 'The Toolkit', where we will look at the tools you need to ensure this is going to be practical and easy to do. We'll look at the kit needed for your home, work bag and office, and advise on things like supplements.

Chapter 10, 'Lifestyle', will look at some of the other habits that support and complement good nutrition, because clearly the world doesn't *completely* revolve around food (!).

And then in Chapter 11 we will focus on how you can take the knowledge from this book and make it happen. We didn't want to just leave you with great information but no plan. That's the worst of all worlds. So the last chapter will help you design your habits so that they stick.

We've designed it to be fairly linear – we suggest you read the first two chapters first, and finish with the last chapter (even if you're not reading it for the first time) because that will help translate information into behaviour change, but the middle sections act more like a reference tool, so you can dip in and out, or cherry-pick the bits you feel are most relevant to your own situation.

Just like with productivity, when you apply a bit of Ninja preparedness, embrace the unorthodox and occasionally even add a little stealth and mindfulness to your food choices, great things happen. And of course, the whole point of a book called *Work Fuel* is to help make it easy to provide rocket fuel for brilliant brains, because the world needs what you do.

We've also prepared a bunch of online PDF resources which you can download and print out, which we'll tell you about when we get to those bits. So, let's dive right in to the nine essentials of the Work Fuel Way.

THE NINE ESSENTIALS OF THE WORK FUEL WAY:

1. BE A FUELIE

GOOD FOOD IS BRAIN FUEL

Let's start with the most obvious thing. 'We are what we eat.' Or rather, our brain performs relative to how well we feed and support it. Our brain and body also need certain vitamins, minerals and macro nutrients to maintain their functions, and good nutrition, hydration and rest are all vital to keep us alert and our attention strong.

Perhaps you describe yourself as a foodie. Perhaps you don't. Either way, we hope with this book we can make you a 'fuelie'. A fuelie is someone who recognizes the benefits of increased energy, lower stress and a healthier body and consciously and consistently makes food choices that support this.

It's important to note, too, that it's just as much about what you don't eat as what you do eat. Set your bar high, make wise choices and your short-term energy will be boosted – not to mention your longer-term health, too.

It doesn't take long to feel the effects either – usually within around two weeks of making these changes, people report better mood, more consistent energy, and confidence. For this to happen though, we must be bothered, interested and aware of what we put into our bodies. So if you're a foodie, we see being a fuelie as a natural upgrade. If you've no interest in being a foodie, and just see food as fuel, then it may as well be rocket fuel!

Since most of us are busy, we cut corners in all of this. It means our brains are tired, starved of certain nutrients, and slightly below our best. The result is that each day we have less of that 'proactive attention' that we talked about earlier. At best, this means we're suboptimal, and at worst this puts us on a path towards exhaustion and burnout. In the middle lies a spectrum of symptoms you'll probably recognize: general tiredness; feeling like you can't concentrate for long periods, especially in the afternoons; getting grumpy or irritable about stupid things; lacking the energy for a social life; not having time or energy for your family; feeling like you just want to stay in bed all day, and so on. These things are not inevitable. You just got so used to them that you forgot that you can change them. A fuelie stays mindful of this and learns how to avoid it altogether.

BRAIN FUEL IS WORK FUEL

When it comes to improving productivity, so many people focus on downloading the latest apps, or buying a new notebook to make pretty lists, when the ultimate tool we need to be taking care of is always with you – right between your ears. Feeding our brains helps us think. And in case you've missed all the Productivity Ninja memos thus far, thinking is the hardest, most valuable, most important work that there is. When the machines come for your job, it's your ability to think, to be creative, to problem-solve and strategize that matters most. The key to great productivity is thinking better. The key to thinking better is eating better.

WORK FUEL *IS LIFE FUEL*

There are many reasons why souped-up productivity is a good thing. We're big fans of the idea of 'playful, productive momentum' throughout all areas of life: the more you embrace positivity in your work, the more it rubs off on your life, and vice versa.

All the stuff we are going to tell you about in this book is just as applicable to life outside of work. Encouraging optimal brain function also means reducing stress and increasing the hormones in your body that produce happiness and feelings of well-being.

The good news is there's no bad news here. Want to have more energy for your kids? Tick. Want to feel better during the dark winter months? That too. Want to perform better in the gym? We've got you. And do you want to do all of this without spending loads more money on food or spending loads more time on prepping it? Don't worry, we'll show you how to make all of this convenient for your time and your bank balance too.

2. LUNCH IS NOT FOR WIMPS

DITCH THE MACHISMO

Gordon Gekko in the famous film *Wall Street* defined the 1980s' high-octane work ethic. 'Lunch is for wimps' was a phrase that cut through into mainstream culture, and you still hear it today. The sad thing is, it's utter nonsense. Deliberately depriving your body and brain the nutrients you need to think properly, and surviving on coffee alone, doesn't make you cool, it just makes you a caffeine-fuelled crazy idiot. It certainly doesn't make you better at your job. It is a sad and empty brag. Of course, there are occasionally days when a lack of planning or a work emergency means you're looking up at the clock at 3pm saying, 'Oh, I forgot to eat'. If that's because you were lost in your work, or on a high-adrenaline deadline, then perhaps you spent the morning being productive. The point is it's unsustainable if you do this regularly – by the second day of skipping lunch, you'll be seriously suboptimal. Let's eliminate this 'lunch is for wimps' rubbish from our culture and fuel our bodies – and our brains – with what they actually need. This macho bragging generally hides average results.

HOW *YOU EAT MATTERS TOO*

There are many useful aspects to the rhythm of how we eat. We're big fans of breakfast because it sets the tone for the day. It's also useful to think of breakfast as the breaking of a fast – it's ideal to have twelve hours during each 24 where you give your body a rest from eating and digesting, so that you can repair and rebuild. (Your sleep time plus avoiding late-evening snacks makes this quite easy when you're in a routine.) These natural mini-fasts are great for digestion. Taking time to enjoy food and eat mindfully, too, allows the body a better chance of absorbing useful nutrients from our food. We digest food properly when the body is relaxed, and the body does the minimum it can get away with when it's highly stressed. The other thing that's often overlooked is chewing. The enzymes we produce as we chew are vital to the digestive process. Eating mindfully and chewing properly aren't luxury extras here, they're vital components of getting optimum energy from what we eat.

DITCH THE 'AL DESKO'

Eating at your desk is bad for you. But you knew that already. There are several productivity reasons that have nothing to do with food – getting even just a few minutes out of the office in the middle of the day is a great way to clear your mind – but aside from this, the ability to move your body into a more relaxed state aids your digestion, and in doing this it enhances the production of energy from your food. So, when you think you don't have twenty minutes for lunch, imagine how many minutes of better energy you're denying yourself by eating at your desk. We'll show you more of the science of this later. For now, consider this: unlike the New York Stock Exchange, the Tokyo Stock Exchange shuts down for a lunch break each day. A study made back in 1999, in Tokyo, analysed the effects of this institutional feature on volatility of stock returns. It clearly showed that the lack of trading over lunch reduces the volatility of the market.[1] Less volatility sounds like a win to us! Take lunch.

3. DON'T EAT FOOD WITH ITS OWN JINGLE

IT'S TIME TO *RECONNECT WITH OUR FOOD*

One of the biggest problems we have in the Western world is that we've become disconnected from what we're eating. Very few people grow any of their own food. Our vegetables arrive already chopped in plastic wrapping, we eat strawberries all year round instead of during their actual season because we can have them flown halfway around the world, and it's hard to know what damage we're doing by eating certain things, because the agricultural processes are so far from our view.

What's happened over the years is that the idea of being healthy has been hijacked by the marketing people. They've recognized that most of us have such a naive understanding of what our food even is that they can adopt a two-step strategy to increase their profits:

1. Tell us something is bad (like saturated fats, gluten, sugar and so on).

2. Tell us their product is low in the thing, or the alternative to the bad thing, and therefore the solution.

And most of us simply don't have the time to investigate the claims of every product. Therefore, we assume products that are low in fat, low in sugars or gluten free must be good for us. We assume that these companies have used science and have our best interests at heart, instead of seeing them as clever people using psychology to sell us often-substandard food. Often these products make up for the thing they leave out by adding in other less desirable ingredients (low-fat foods, for example, are often much higher in sugar).

So, we need to reconnect with food. A good rule of thumb is: if food needs a marketing team to convince us it's worth eating, it's probably not worth eating.

Steer clear of the jingles. There's a reason you never see a humble broccoli singing in an advertisement.

FOOD MADE FROM PLANTS, NOT FOOD MADE IN PLANTS

Another simple rule is this one. Eat more food made *from* plants, not food made *in* plants. Factories need to include additives and preservatives to give food a long shelf life, they use cooking or manufacturing techniques that cut corners, which both ultimately reduce the nutritional value. Vegetables are one of the simplest ways to get a lot of nutrition quickly and should be thought of as a major part of a meal, not a little side-show next to the main event. We'll show you how to give your plate a 'plant slant'.

4. EAT THE RAINBOW

One of the simplest ways to ensure your plate is full of nutrients is to look at the colours. Obviously, we've all heard of 'eat your greens', but what about all those reds, yellows, purples and oranges? Different-coloured vegetables tend to contain different nutrients, so a rainbow on your plate will help ensure you're not missing anything out. If you look at the finger food options at a big event like a wedding or conference, what you'll generally see is a whole lot of beige. The meat is so processed it's beige, the pastries are beige, there are a lot of potato or bread-based products (fried or processed), melted cheese and so on. Thankfully things are starting to improve as more people start to demand more varied options.

BANISH *THE BEIGE*

The same beige-complex is true for the freezer section of most supermarkets, where the pre-prepared meals are generally heavily processed and pumped full of refined salt and flavourings to make sure they taste good after the freeze. If, like us, you grew up on potato waffles, crispy pancakes and the like, you'll be familiar with what we mean. Some of those foods with cartoon characters and jingles remind us of childhood and can bring feelings of comfort, but getting beyond the beige is a quick-fire step to better energy.

RANGE

As you'll hear in the next chapter, it's important to eat a wide range of good foods, yet it's easy to find yourself stuck in a pattern of eating the same four meals over and over again. 'Eat the rainbow' reminds us to focus on range – both on an individual plate and over the course of a day or a week. This doesn't necessarily mean you need a massive repertoire of dishes to cook: simply adding a handful of something colourful to an existing dish to 'rainbow it up' is enough to extend your range. Baby tomatoes, pre-chopped carrots or salad, a bit of sauerkraut or beetroot out of a jar … these things are all easy to add to a plate in a few seconds and yet they all add extra colour, flavour and nutrition to whatever else you're eating.

5. BE LABEL-SAVVY

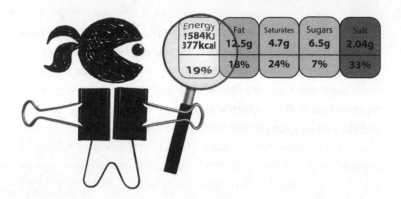

Energy 1584KJ 377kcal	Fat	Saturates	Sugars	Salt
	12.5g	4.7g	6.5g	2.04g
19%	18%	24%	7%	33%

We talked about reconnecting with food. Getting to know its prov-
enance, and what some of the marketing-speak does and doesn't
mean, can be time-consuming. Luckily for you we've created a whole
chapter here – Chapter 6 – with some quick things you can do to
make better food choices. One or two of the things in that chapter
may shock you. In particular, this next thing.

STOP COUNTING CALORIES

Calories aren't the smartest measure for fuel for a human body, and
we don't actually burn them in the way that is shouted about by
every new workout programme. It's a bit of a waste of time counting them at all. For example, a hundred calories from a packet of
crisps is simply different from a hundred calories from a handful of
walnuts. The way our body reacts, metabolizes, utilizes and feels is
different. This is due to the macro and micro nutrients contained in
each food; the walnut is much more nutritionally balanced than a
packet of crisps, and so are we when we eat it. Our society tends to
equate calories with health, which is just wrong. Would you rather

eat 2,000 calories a day of densely packed, healthy and nutritious food, or 2,000 calories made entirely of fries? Which would leave you feeling at your best?

What is a calorie anyway? Technically, it's the measure of how much energy it takes to heat up water by a single degree. It's an old and arbitrary way to think about the energy from food. What's much more important to understand is something called adenosine triphosphate – ATP – which is the energy currency of our bodies, and they need a range of nutrients to create it. None of these processes are explained by a calorie. Much better to count colours of the rainbow in your meal, or simply focus on eating well in line with the Work Fuel Plate (more of which in the next chapter) and forget counting calories altogether. Phew.

THE FIVE-INGREDIENT RULE

Another quick rule of thumb when you look at the label on anything in a packet is to just count the ingredients – the ideal is under five. If you look at organic porridge oats, it will usually say 'Ingredients: organic porridge oats'. That's it. One ingredient. One-ingredient foods are generally good for you, because they're the source food and they don't contain additives that can slow down or even inhibit the nutrients from the original ingredient. Once you start getting into a long list of 'emulsifiers' and 'flavour agents' you know it was made in a plant. Think about some of these names: 'ammonium sulphate', for example. Seen often as E517, it is used as an acidity regulator in bread, but scarily is also used in agricultural sprays such as water-soluble insecticides, herbicides and fungicides. Or 'titanium dioxide', used in foods to make them whiter. This is a component of the metal titanium, commonly used in paints and sunscreens. Plus, it's mined and may contain traces of lead. What about 'hydrolysed gluten', and the famous and ubiquitous 'high-fructose corn syrup'? What even *are* they? When was the last time you walked past a hydrolysed gluten tree? Things that don't grow naturally are, as a rule of thumb, not the best things to give you optimal energy.

YOU'RE SWEET ENOUGH

Sugar is added to many more products than you'd expect. Sure, it's in the burger buns of McDonald's hamburgers and it's one of the major ingredients of most ketchup sauces. But even seemingly healthier options like regular loaves of bread, granola, breakfast cereals, protein bars and low-fat yoghurts will contain large amounts of added sugar. A lot of fruit juices even have added sugar, on top of all the natural fruit sugars they already contain. Sugar addiction is easy to spot when it's chocolate bars and sweets that you're craving but added sugars might be the reason you're drawn to certain foods without realizing it.

6. BE NINJA PREPARED

One of the common problems with trying to lead a healthier lifestyle is that we're busy. It can be hard to find easy, convenient options that are also nutritious. Being on the move also means we're away from our own kitchens and can easily fall prey to convenient but suboptimal choices. When you've been working all day, it's late and you're tired in a city you don't know well, your willpower is down and your propensity to succumb to the food made in factories is sky high. Ninja preparedness is all about thinking ahead, avoiding those scenarios as much as possible. Just like productivity-related preparedness, it can feel like a 'luxury' activity ('but I don't have *time* to be boxing up salad at 7am when I need to catch a train!'). We get that. It can also feel a little bit too much like the Scouts. And no one wants that. In fact, our own personal styles – with productivity as much as in life – lean towards 'going with the flow' more than 'being prepared' and we've learnt to force ourselves into a little more neatness and structure. What's helped us to do this is to think of being prepared as giving your future self a little gift ...

▶ *These ten minutes of genius preparation now will save me a load of time (and often a load of money too!) at lunchtime today.*

▶ *This little bit of information-gathering here when I'm more relaxed will help my future self, who is in the middle of a work day and probably, er, much less relaxed.*

▶ *This one big effort creates points of ease and easy solutions for days on end.*

EATING WELL IS EASY *WHEN YOU MAKE IT EASY*

One of Graham's biggest learnings when Colette was coaching him was her saying 'You eat well when you've got good stuff in your fridge.' Graham doesn't have a wide cooking repertoire, yet when you think about it, you don't really need hundreds of recipes to eat well. Once he started loading the fridge with the right ingredients, the kind of meals he was able to send to Colette on the WhatsApp chat looked much like the ones Colette sent back. Graham had mistakenly thought he needed to be a chef. Really, he just needed to be a 'home kitchen stock manager' – which is much easier.

Eating well is easy when you make it easy. One of the hardest places to eat well is when you're on a long-haul flight or a train journey when all you have is the limited outlets to purchase from, or even worse, the salt-and-chemical-injected food they give you on board. Staying hydrated is hard if you're having to be the nuisance passenger asking for water every half an hour, or worse still, the one getting ripped off buying plastic bottles of water for a small fortune because they know you don't have another option. Make your future self happy by making these scenarios so much easier – we'll show you how.

WORK OUT YOUR SOFT SPOTS

As you'll hear, we're not particularly tight-laced about what you should eat. If you like a Mars bar every now and then, so what? If you're partial to a tiramisu when you're out for dinner, then good for you. These can be occasional treats and they don't do you much harm. The problem comes if you're regularly making the same choices. If you're having a Mars bar every time you get petrol, and every day you're in the office at 4pm, and every time you're bored, then it becomes something of a soft spot. If you swap a proper lunch for a Snickers and a bag of crisps once because all hell broke loose that day, well it's not ideal but it's not going to kill you. If you're doing that several days a week you are compromising your performance, energy and health. Knowing your soft spots is one of the first places to start when it comes to being prepared. If you can reflect and think about what your consistent bad choices are, then you can start to plan to make it easier to make a better choice next time those scenarios arrive.

Preparedness is always about giving a gift to your future self. Don't leave your future self in the lurch, because your future self will be as busy that day as you are now, and needs the help. Help your future self to be well equipped to make the best quality choices – and you'll give yourself more energy and build better habits as a result.

7. CHOOSE CONSISTENCY OVER INTENSITY

In evaluating your lifestyle choices, remember it's not what you did today, it's what you generally do that matters. It's all about balance. Too many people think that detoxing in January makes up for eleven months of indulgence. And too many people also feel guilty when they have a coffee with marshmallows, even though they've been filling their body with nutrient-packed food all week. It's time to get some balance here. It's time to celebrate the undervalued virtue of quiet consistency.

We are bombarded by the opposite of quiet consistency – fasting! Biohacking! Ketosis! No carbs! Detox like Beyoncé! Extreme this, revolutionize that. All these things promise quick fixes to complex problems. They tickle our desires for immediate results and low effort. In truth, the consistency of how we live our everyday lives matters much more than the intensity of what we do in the few short moments our motivation is at its height.

STEER CLEAR OF THE FADS

As a rule, avoid fad diets and food regimes. Remember, this is not a diet or weight loss book. It's about eating consistently well to fuel your brain. If you have other things you need to fix (and we're talking health issues here, not the need for a flatter stomach!) then there might be a case for a more rigid and regimented food plan. For the rest of us, what's more likely is that you'll have two weeks of feeling highly motivated, following the new plan, and then slowly but surely the wheels will fall off and you're back to square one. The real danger of fad diets is that they leave us back where we started, but actually less motivated than before, because we 'tried that other diet and it didn't make me healthier'. It's also confusing. Over 80% of people claim that today's conflicting dietary advice makes it harder than ever to choose what to eat.[2]

Fad diet plans tend to have an end date. 'Be beach ready in four weeks!' This suggests that you follow their plan for a month, and then that's it, everything will be perfect. But we all know that this just isn't the case – you can't go to the gym and lift a weight for a month and expect to be buff forever. You have to go back time and time again to see the improvements, maintain the habit, lift heavier weights, mix it up and refine it. Only then will you see and feel the benefit that keeps you motivated, going back time after time.

FORGIVE YOURSELF

Let's address the issue of guilt. Many people never feel guilty about what they eat, but for a lot of people, eating certain foods can bring intense emotions. We might feel comfort, because that food tastes so good, or reminds us of a time in our childhood, and then we might feel a bit guilty afterwards that it wasn't a good choice. This book aims to be a guilt-free space. Don't beat yourself up. All you can do is your best and if your best today is a supermarket-bought sandwich, then we can deal with that and move on. Do the small things consistently and well, and do you know what? It's not the end of the world. It's not what you did today, it's what you do most days that counts.

THE MICRO BEATS THE MACRO, *THE TORTOISE BEATS THE HARE*

Just as with productivity, the life-changing habits are formed from the mundane. The macro, headline stuff is sexy, but it's in the trenches of day-to-day life that we develop the habits that slowly but surely change our behaviour. And do you know what? All those tiny changes are harder than making a bold leap to full-blast detox in the hope that you might keep it up. You've probably come across the four stages of competence, which is a model that describes how we learn and develop new habits and skills. It's the journey through:

▶ Unconscious incompetence (we can't do it, and don't know how)

▶ Conscious incompetence (we start to see our failings)

▶ Conscious competence (we can do it, but it takes an almighty effort to keep it on track)

▶ Unconscious competence (effortless, habitual mastery).

The hardest part of developing new habits, especially with something as central to both our physical well-being and our daily routines, is the conscious competence. That's the moment where we're experimenting with a new habit, applying willpower, and working it all out. It's hard to challenge our old habits. There might be times when you're scared to try new things, or it just feels like you don't have the headspace. But it's the slow and steady that wins in the end. And the way to become the tortoise rather than the hare is to have patience in the beginning, challenge yourself to make changes outside of your comfort zone, and watch them become a sustainable part of your everyday life. It starts with a great breakfast and gets better from there.

8. THINK NUTRIFUL **BEFORE BEAUTIFUL**

YOUR FOOD IS FUEL, AND IT DOESN'T NEED TO BE ON INSTAGRAM

Over the past few years, society has glamourized food to the point of fetish. Look at the range of large-format, full-colour cookbooks on the shelves of your local bookshop, or in the Amazon top twenty, and you'll see what we mean. It seems society has decided that lettuce is only good for you if it's got that seductive, moist sheen dripping from it. And it's got to be symmetrical, obviously! Imagine how it would taste if it wasn't symmetrical! All this perfection is paralysing for some of us and can stop us giving cooking and food prep a chance.

We prefer to focus on 'nutriful', not beautiful. The point is that you can throw together nourishing, tasty ingredients into a salad bowl in less than five minutes. Some of the veggie curries Graham makes look brown and horrible, quite frankly, but they're packed full of goodness, taste great and are made from a rainbow plate of raw ingredients, of course! Life is not a dinner party. You don't have to see a beautiful plate every time you sit down to eat. Far better to see a nutriful plate of food every time you eat.

Jamie Oliver is Britain's second biggest-selling author after J.K. Rowling. Yet while we consume his, and Gwyneth's and Nigella's books, too few of us are actually doing any cooking. According to a recent study, Britons now spend more than five hours a week consuming 'food media' – but only four hours actually cooking.[3]

Some of these books are just not helpful, often falsely using the term 'easy' or giving a 'minutes' promise, assuming a whole load of kit and expertise, with beautifully displayed but unrealistic results, not to mention ingredients that are difficult to source. This is disabling rather than enabling, so we think what matters is getting back to basics and de-complicating a simple topic – cooking.

Of course, if your plate looks beautiful as well as nutriful, that's fine! But don't underestimate the power of social media, advertising and peer pressure. Your weird homemade wrap with its badly cut bits of avocado is no less tasty or nutritious than the pretty one you bought from the fancy sandwich shop yesterday. Beautiful might come later, but don't make it the focus. Just cook. Eat great ingredients. Allow for the imperfection.

9. HUMAN NOT SUPERHERO

A Productivity Ninja is not superhuman, but may sometimes appear to be so. Yes, being a Productivity Ninja can leave your colleagues marvelling (excuse the pun) at your extreme productivity and they might even confer on you superhero status. But the truth is far simpler. A Productivity Ninja is just a human being with a great skill set – all that zen-like calm, ruthlessness, weapon-saviness, agility and preparedness can take you a long way. Yet beneath all of that, they're still human. And humans are fallible, imperfect and – let's be honest here – usually a little bit weird.

There is a huge freedom that comes from embracing the fact that we are human: we don't need to *do* or *be* everything, we have permission to screw things up sometimes and we don't need to be embarrassed to associate ourselves with our own flaws and foibles. In fact, acknowledging when we're stuck, when we're struggling to break free from old habits, or when we don't have the confidence to do what we know is needed is a much quicker way of solving these things than trying to be a superhero (and then realizing you can't actually fly or beat off your procrastination with special powers).

DON'T USE UP YOUR WILLPOWER *AT HOME*

Of course, a big part of eating right is having the willpower. We'll focus later in the book, in Chapter 11, on how we make habits stick, how we use our willpower wisely, and why willpower is a depleting resource each day. That's right: however well intentioned you may be, you have a limited amount of willpower. Yes, you can train your brain to develop more willpower, but it's always limited. So rather than starting by aiming for perfection (unsustainable), let's focus on minimizing the slip-ups. Much more realistic.

So, here's a quick one for starters. Don't use your willpower at home. It's the place you spend the most time, so don't give yourself choices to make. We are both people who, if we have biscuits in the cupboard, will hear those biscuits calling our name until they're all gone. Usually on the day we bought them. And do you know how we get around that? We don't let them into the house in the first place! Same goes for other tempting snacks or meals that aren't nutriful. Then we are not using all that willpower every time we enter the kitchen to make a cuppa, or every time we're putting a meal together. What that also means is that you have more of your willpower left for the occasions where it's even more difficult – when you're on the move, standing next to the vending machine, or at the counter buying a coffee and the muffin is calling you.

THE CLEVER, MOTIVATED YOU *VS THE LAZY, SCATTERBRAINED YOU*

All of this comes down to an internal battle that we face in our brains every day. The angel on one shoulder, the devil on the other. In *How to be a Study Ninja* Graham referred to this as the Lazy, Scatterbrained You and the Clever, Motivated You. They are both you. And as hunting animals that no longer need to hunt for survival, we will spend much more of our thinking in the lazy, scatterbrained part of our brain. Kick back. Relax. Think about it all later.

If it were a boxing match, we'd see the lazy, scatterbrained thinking making its constant jabs. What we often need in those situations is one big sucker-punch from the clever, motivated part of our brain. Walking straight past the biscuit section in the supermarket will avoid hundreds of little jabs from the lazy, scatterbrained part of you ('Go on. Have another biscuit. Have so many that you don't need a meal. Go on.'). Small habits are often formed by those big moments of truth.

THIS IS THE WORK FUEL WAY

This isn't a cookbook. It isn't a diet plan. It's about how to live life with more energy, making informed daily choices that fuel your body, not just for a few weeks, but sustainably for the rest of your days. What's more, all of these choices also support health and well-being. You might say that should go without saying, but actually, certain diet plans and weird biohacking regimes can in fact have the opposite result in the long term. Here, there's no choice to be made between your health and getting maximum energy. It's a big win-win. You're going to like most of what you hear in these next chapters. And occasionally we're probably going to annoy you too. Usually, to be fair, with some scientific data to back us up. We encourage you to jump head first into all of this, and to focus equally on what you're drawn to and what you're repelled by. That way, you'll make the easy changes as well as challenge yourself to get outside your comfort zone.

Are you a Ninja?

▶ A Ninja knows that attention – rather than time – is our most precious resource. And the best way to deal with our 'proactive attention' being in such short supply? Eat well so that you create more of it.

▶ A Ninja adopts the mindset set out in the nine essentials of the Work Fuel Way, thinking like a fuelie, taking lunch seriously, and making smart food choices.

▶ A Ninja may sometimes appear like they're a superhero, but deep down we know that a Ninja is simply a human being, albeit one with a great mindset and skills. As humans, we allow ourselves the odd slip-up and imperfection. So sometimes we have cake.

2.
FOOD FOR THOUGHT: NUTRITION FOR COGNITION AND THE WORK FUEL PLATE

EVER WISH THERE WAS AN EXTRA DAY IN YOUR WEEK?

We all want to maximize our brain power and increase our energy levels, but what if we told you that eating certain foods would give you 26% extra executive decision-making power? That's more than an extra day of brain power every working week.[1]

In this chapter we're going to show you some of the science and research so you can see what makes a difference and why. And then to make it practical, we'll introduce you to a key tool, the Work Fuel Plate, which will be our visual guide for what to eat.

A BIT OF NEUROSCIENCE

Neurotransmission is the process that commands how we think, feel and react on a day-to-day basis. It requires the correct and appropriate creation of the various brain chemicals, known as neurotransmitters, to enable transmission along the neurons and between the neurons. An example of a neurotransmitter is serotonin, the happiness hit, or dopamine, which has a boosting effect, providing drive, energy, focus and a mood lift. These neurotransmitters are made from – you've guessed it – our food.

On days when you feel sluggish, that feeling is likely caused by your brain chemistry being starved of what it needs to operate. The food we eat is broken down into nutrients, which are picked up by the bloodstream and dropped off at the brain to support cellular reactions, top up daily levels of critical nutrients and, most importantly, build brain tissue.

Let's look at an example – tryptophan. Tryptophan is an essential amino acid (one of the building blocks of protein that we can only get from our diet) and it's required for the production of serotonin. It's found in many protein-rich foods, such as chia seeds, pumpkin seeds, turkey, fish, beans, avocados, lentils, nuts, natural yoghurt, and eggs. If we don't eat foods with tryptophan daily, we may produce less serotonin, making it much harder for the brain to stay optimistic and focused. In an experiment carried out by the psychiatry department at the College of Medicine, Korea, healthy volunteers found that the effects of lowered tryptophan included lowered mood, memory impairment and an increase in aggression.[2] Our levels of serotonin are also quite responsive to sugar highs and lows.

When Colette was coaching Graham, one of his biggest revelations was on the importance of tryptophan. Graham was suffering from low moods and low energy during the dark English winter, but found that including more foods containing tryptophan, alongside other changes, alleviated his symptoms within a few weeks.

FEED THE BRAIN, FUEL ITS PERFORMANCE

'Our brains literally are what we eat.'
– Dr Lisa Mosconi

Protein from foods such as meat, fish and eggs is the backbone of our brain cells. Carbohydrates, such as glucose from fruit, vegetables and whole grains, energize the brain. Fats are broken down into fatty acids to make our neurons flexible and responsive, support our immune system, and shield the brain from damage.

The good news is that the brain reacts quite quickly to what we feed it. An investigation by Weill Cornell Medicine in 2018 showed that longer-term brain-healthy eating patterns are key to successful ageing.[3] The investigation showed a scan of the brain activity of two 50-year-old women: one who ate a Mediterranean-style diet (one rich in vegetables, fruit, nuts and seeds, whole grains, herbs and spices, fish and seafood, and extra virgin olive oil) and one who ate a Western-style diet (one rich in red meat, dairy products, processed and artificially sweetened foods, and salt, with minimal intake of fruit, vegetables, fish, legumes and whole grains).

The woman with a Western-style diet showed substantially lower brain activity than her counterpart on the scan. The study was underpinned by further research published in the *British Medical Journal* and *Neurology*. In both these studies it was found that patients who ate a Mediterranean-style diet exhibited fewer Alzheimer's-related changes to their brains than those who ate a Western-style diet.[4]

Crucially they demonstrated that the micro choices we make each day have the potential to massively affect our brain activity, providing us with better productivity and focus and better general health – it all depends on these daily choices.[5]

WHAT EXACTLY SHOULD WE EAT

So let's get into the practical bit. What exactly should we be eating to give us the best chance of optimal nutrition and energy? We know you're busy, and we're fans of simple visual guides, so allow us to introduce the Work Fuel Plate.

'Every time you eat or drink, you are either feeding disease or fighting it.'
– Heather Morgan

The Work Fuel Plate is made up of three core ingredients: rainbow plants, protein and smarter carbs. You'll have noticed that there are three supplementary ingredients featured too, which are crucial to the Work Fuel formula. These are fats, fermented foods and hydration. It's important to note that the supplementary ingredients can often be found within the core ingredients, and vice versa. For example, avocados, a plant, are made up of 85% fat. Eating one is both topping up your rainbow and getting a good helping of fat. Similarly, yoghurt is a good source of protein which not only contains around 4% fat but is also a fermented food.

THE *WORK FUEL PLATE*

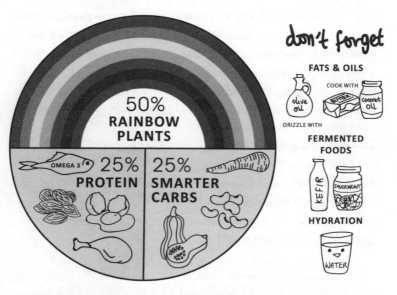

Print a colour version at **www.workfuel.ninja/plate**

In the case of hydration you will need to add this in throughout the day. Water is best consumed away from mealtimes. Sipping during a meal is fine, just try to avoid gulping down multiple glasses with food, as it may slow digestion. The aim is to adopt Ninja mindfulness, so that you can quickly scan, pick or plan a plate to set yourself up for more success.

CORE INGREDIENT NO. 1: RAINBOW PLANTS

How much? Fifty per cent of the plate or two big handfuls, more whenever you can!

'Eat food. Not too much. Mostly plants.'
– Michael Pollan

The quote above is taken from an article in the *New York Times*, 'Unhappy Meals'. Pollan is an American author, journalist, activist and professor of journalism. As a result of his decades of research into food and dietary patterns, he says that, more or less, this quote is the short answer to the sup-posedly incredibly complicated and confusing question of what we humans should eat in order to be maximally healthy. By food he means real food, not the processed varieties we have become accustomed to, and as for plants, well, let's explore that in a little more detail here.

Take a plant slant on your plate

Eat the rainbow is an essential of the Work Fuel Way. Each different-coloured food has a different nutrient profile, so simply different health benefits. We just can't afford to be picky with these, we need to eat all of them. For example, the nutrient lutein is a carotenoid (a yellow pigment found in food), and it's an incredibly import-ant nutrient for our vision and cognition. We can't make it in the body and so we have to find it from foods. Lutein is only found in foods that have a natural yellow pigment – yellow peppers, green veggies, bananas, egg yolk … you get the idea. Purple foods then have another unique set of nutritional gifts for us, such as antho-cyanins – an antioxidant that's shown promising results in improving

cognitive performance.[6] Red, pink, green foods all have other nutrients that support different mechanisms in the body.

> ● **REMEMBER THIS** ●
>
> **Antioxidants:** These help to prevent or stop cell damage
> caused by oxidants. Get it? *Anti-oxidants*. Oxidants can be from
> your environment (for example, air pollution), but they're also
> produced naturally in your body (e.g. during stress). The body
> needs a balance of antioxidants and oxidants, and as you can
> imagine these days this balance is often slightly skewed in the
> direction of the oxidants. Antioxidants are primarily found in
> plant-based foods.

The more vibrant the colour, the more potential gifts a food contains, so if we are going to be super strategic, let's really hone in on
the VIPs:

Enter the Very Important Plants – the real VIPs

Tomatoes   Tomatoes contain an antioxidant called lycopene, which
helps to protect fats, proteins and DNA from the damage caused
by free radicals (energy-deficient molecules that steal energy from
other cells, harming them in the process). Left unchecked, free-
radical damage increases the risk of premature ageing, heart disease
and cognitive decline. Observational studies suggest a correlation
between people diagnosed with mild cognitive impairment and
low blood levels of lycopene and other carotenoids. Lycopene is
also involved in the regulation of genes that influence inflammation
in the brain.[7]

Tomatoes are more nutritious when cooked instead of raw as the
lycopene content is more bioavailable. The cooking process helps
to break down cell membranes that trap lycopene and as a result
more lycopene is available for the body to absorb. Think tomato
soup, roasted tomatoes and tomato-based pasta sauces.

Broccoli   Broccoli contains sulforaphane, a compound that, studies show, plays an important role in preventing brain age-ing.[8] It helps to fortify and repair the blood-brain barrier following damage. This barrier protects the brain from potentially harmful chemicals and toxins in the blood. The compound is found in its highest concentration in raw broccoli – when it's cooked or frozen the sulforaphane is lost. However, there are a couple of things you can do to offset this. Chop fresh broccoli an hour before you are going to cook it – the compound is then allowed to fully form and is retained during cooking. Or just cook it and add mustard to the finished dish. Mustard contains an enzyme that re-activates the lost compound (and it tastes great, too).[9] Broccoli is also packed with antioxidants that are retained in cooking. These include vita-min C to protect against free-radical damage, and vitamins B and K to enhance memory function.[10] One of the B vitamins, called choline, is closely associated with healthy brain development and maintenance.[11]

Beetroot   Beetroot contains high concentrations of nitrates that help to dilate blood vessels and boost circulation. Improved blood flow means improved brain function.[12] In fact, nitrates have been shown to enhance circulation to the brain's frontal lobe, an area related to executive functioning. Nitrates can also be found in other vegetables such as carrots, rocket, radishes and cabbage.[13]

Avocados   You get two for one when you eat an avocado: a colour for your rainbow and a dose of brain-friendly fat too (see Supplementary Ingredient No. 1 for more on this). They are also rich in vitamin E and in one of the carotenoids – lutein – that we have already mentioned, along with zeaxanthin (LZ). LZ has been shown to improve visual processing speed and to enhance cognitive func-tion, learning, memory, concentration and focus. It is found in many other sources, such as dark leafy greens, yellow fruits and egg yolk.

However, the avocado delivers it in a perfect fat pack, which means it is more easily absorbed by the body.[14]

> ● **REMEMBER THIS** ●
>
> Home late or up early, avocado is a go-to mini meal. Just slice open, add a bit of salt, lemon or chilli – and voila! They are known for taking a long time to ripen and a short time to go bad. Top tip: as soon as they are ripe, either eat them or chop them in half, remove the skin and freeze. Frozen avocado works perfectly in guacamole and smoothies.

Dark Leafy Greens Eat your greens. You probably remember your mum giving you this advice when you were young. It was good advice, although more accurately for the purpose of this book we would like to advise you to eat your *dark leafy* greens. The dark leafy greens like rocket, watercress, spinach, kale, romaine lettuce and cabbage are rich in folate. This is an essential nutrient in the methylation cycle, which plays a huge part in bodily functions such as energy production and mood control. Poor methylation is linked with a variety of diseases including Alzheimer's. When methylation is working and aligned, it's like a successful corporate strategy, where everything else seems to be magically moving in the right direction. But when methylation is struggling, the rest of your body is like a team with no motivation.

So from now on, to please your mum if nothing else, eat your *dark leafy* greens!

Blueberries Blueberries have one of the highest antioxidant values of all foods and are also very low in fructose (sugars) compared to other fruits. Blend into smoothies or sprinkle on top of your morning porridge; eat as a snack, or have a bag of berries on the go in your freezer – great in the summer as an alternative to sugary ice lollies and perfect for adding to smoothies and warm dishes in the winter.

Berries contain powerful antioxidants that stimulate blood flow and oxygen delivery to the brain, protect against damage and inflammation, and improve the communication between neurons. There is emerging evidence that these antioxidants support short-term memory and coordination and may also delay age-related cognitive decline.

> ● REMEMBER THIS ●
>
> Focus on eating more veggies than fruit (maximum two to three portions of fruit per day, 80 g each, equal to a medium-sized apple or banana). Veggies have less sugar. Fruits grown in temperate climates like the UK are exposed to less sun, which means less sugar. Eating fruits where you can eat the skin, like cherries, apples and berries, means you eat more fibre, promoting blood sugar balance.

CORE INGREDIENT NO. 2: PROTEIN

Eating protein with each meal gives our brain the building blocks to create brain cells, keeps us fuller for longer, and makes us happier. Generally, we tend to under-consume protein until lunch and then overdo it in the evening, when it's actually better to get it in earlier and have a more even spread throughout the day as it contributes to that early-in-the-day blood sugar management that often sets the tone of our appetite for the rest of the day.[15]

How much? Twenty-five per cent of your plate. This equates roughly to a palm-sized amount from an animal source (e.g. meat and fish) or two handfuls from plant-based sources (e.g. lentils, beans, etc.). How much protein we need depends on which study you read and how physically active you are. There are ranges of different guidelines with specific weights, but they are just that – guidelines. We are never going to ask you to weigh stuff. We're too busy to bother with this on a typical work day, and we assume you are too.

> ● **REMEMBER THIS** ●
>
> Protein is one of the three macro nutrients required by the human body; the other two are carbohydrates and fat. These are things that personal trainers, athletes and bodybuilders talk about a lot – getting their 'macros' right, to achieve a certain goal. It's very individual. The Work Fuel Plate is a simplified guide to these proportions for our purposes, but sometimes some people need more of one thing than another; there is not one precise size that fits all.

Protein, or more accurately the amino acids that protein is made up of, slow down the rate at which the stomach empties its food, creating a feeling of being full up. In slowing the rate of digestion, it also helps with the control of insulin, so balancing blood sugar and therefore stabilizing your energy levels and mood and helping to avoid ups and downs. There is a direct link between our mood and blood sugar balance. The more out of kilter your blood sugar is, the more unbalanced your mood. Ever been 'hangry' and then felt sorry afterwards? Yeah, us too.

When we think of protein, we tend to think of meat and animal products, but there is a whole range of other sources out there: nuts, seeds, beans, legumes – even green veggies contain it. In the five regions of the world where people live the longest, the communities there tend to eat meat just once per week and fish maybe twice. The single food common denominator across all those regions is beans, and they eat those every day![16]

Be an egghead!

You've probably heard the term 'egghead' to describe a smart person. Well, perhaps it's partly due to the fact that eggs improve neural processing speed, memory and learning. By design they contain everything needed to grow a new brain. This makes eggs

– especially the yolks – perfect work fuel (no egg-white omelettes for us!). They literally contain a little bit of nearly every vitamin and mineral required by a human being. For example, eggs are an abundant source of choline: a study in 2011 demonstrated that a higher choline intake was related to better overall cognitive performance, specifically a sharper memory.[17] Please don't worry about the dietary cholesterol and your heart, either. Thankfully, recent long-term studies have even suggested that egg consumption lowers markers for cardiovascular disease.

Enjoy eggs a few times a week as one of your protein sources and buy organic if you can. Aside from the fact that the chickens are treated more humanely (worth the cost in our minds immediately), the nutrient profile is so much better and there's less of the nasties like antibiotics, hormones and other pharmaceuticals.[18]

Sources of Protein

Meat   Choose the best quality you can source. Look for terms like local, free-range, grass-fed and organic on the label. Here's a frightening thought to illustrate why: it's not just 'we are what we eat', but more precisely, 'we are what the animals we eat have eaten'. Intensive farming methods result in the animals being injected with antibiotics and hormones, being fed an unnatural diet sometimes dosed with preservatives. The better-quality meat is more pricey, but for good reason, so eat a little less and reap the benefits. It goes without saying that it's better for the animals and the planet too.

Fish and seafood   Choose SMASH fish when you can: **s**ardines, **m**ackerel, **a**nchovies, **s**almon and **h**erring. These fish are high in the brain-friendly omega-3 fat. As a general rule the smaller fish – the size that will fit on a plate head to tail – are more sustainable too. The Marine Stewardship Council (MSC) have a blue label with the letters MSC for fish and seafood in the UK; it's only awarded to sustainable production.[19] Look out for it, or the equivalent in your country, as the non-farmed, sustainable fish are a great inclusion in your diet two or three times per week, in a palm-sized portion.

Pulses, legumes and grains   There are so many to choose from, and the more variety you include the better: lentils, quinoa, chick-peas and all of the brilliant beans: aduki, butter, borlotti, flageolet, haricot, pinto, cannellini, edamame and mung (all also great sources of smarter carbs, so no need for extra carbs if you have these on your plate). A couple of handfuls will ensure you have a good serving of protein each meal.

Nuts and seeds   Take your pick of a handful of these protein- and fat-rich goodies per day: almonds; hazelnuts; cashews; walnuts; pine; brazil, pecan and macadamia nuts, and hemp, sunflower, pumpkin, sesame and flax seeds.

Dairy products   Milk, cheese, yoghurt and cow's milk kefir are all nutritious inclusions on the Work Fuel Plate. Just like with meat, it's worth spending the extra here and buying organic if you can, to help avoid antibiotics and other nasties.[20] It increases the fatty acid profile in favour of the omega-3s, which is priceless when it comes to brain power. See page 52 for the details on this.

Goat's and sheep's milk products are great alternatives too, espe-cially if you are sensitive to dairy, as they are usually better tolerated, as are fermented dairy products, like yoghurt. The bacteria break down the large protein molecules and sugars to some extent, thereby facilitating our digestion a little. Portion-wise, a piece of cheese should be the size roughly of half a square Post-it note and as thick as your thumb (a little more if fresh like mozzarella or cottage cheese) and eaten two or three times per week. Milk and yoghurt can feature daily but think a cup-sized amount. Good options are fresh cheeses like buffalo mozzarella, feta and ricotta; fermented cheeses like Jarlsberg and goat's; or strong-tasting cheeses like Parmesan, where you need only a little to make a big impact. Increasingly people are dropping dairy from their diet for ethical or digestive reasons. Sometimes this relates to intensive farming concerns. The alternative plant milks (sometimes referred to as mylks), yoghurts and cheese-style products have much lower levels of protein, hence they are not itemized here. We can easily get protein from other sources if dairy is not an option; it's just useful to be aware of this.

Soya protein Made from the soya bean, soya protein products are an important plant source of protein. When choosing soya foods, pay attention to quality as many include nasty additives and flavourings. Traditional Asian cultures provide a model of how to best consume it. They consume mainly *fermented* soya products, or tofu in small amounts, but not as their only source of protein.

Fermentation makes soybeans more digestible, as naturally they are hard to digest. It also adds flavour. Tofu isn't fermented, but it tends to be easier to digest because of the way it's made. Edamame are the green, young soybeans. They are high in fibre and protein, sold fresh or frozen, and they are great for topping up the protein content or adding colour to a dish.

More highly processed soy foods such as burgers and products with isolated soy protein or soy flour are best avoided or eaten only very occasionally. Like other highly processed foods, these are likely to have their own jingle and colourful labels with health claims. But they are hard to digest and may even block the absorption of other nutrients.

Plant proteins   If you eat a plant-only diet it's even more import-ant to mix up the protein sources, as only a few sources in the plant world are what are known as complete proteins. To be considered 'complete', a protein must contain the nine essential amino acids, in roughly equal amounts. All animal proteins are complete, and a few plant sources are too – quinoa, hemp seed, chia seeds, buckwheat and spirulina (blue-green algae). This isn't a big problem though, as we tend to mix them up naturally anyhow – think peanut butter on toast, or hummus and wholemeal pitta bread, or brown rice with beans. All of these create a complete set; just mix up your plant sources of protein each day.

CORE INGREDIENT NO. 3: SMARTER CARBS

How much? Twenty-five per cent of the plate.

Are you avoiding or scared of carbs? Contrary to the current zeit-geist, bread isn't necessarily the bad guy. Carbohydrates are fuel and have a significant role to play in our diets. Even the super-strict 'no carb' diets incorporate these foods back into the diet again at some point. Tryptophan – remember the precursor to serotonin? (Of course you did) – needs carbohydrate in order to be absorbed, so eating foods with some carbs boosts serotonin production.[21] It's just a matter of choosing 'smarter' carbs over the dumber variety that are low in nutrition.

The innocent-looking dumb carbs are the ones we usually consume on a regular basis – white rice, pasta, pastries and bread. They have sadly been dumbed down through refining. Ironically, refining normally means making something better, but in this case it's the opposite. The process of refining a food not only removes the fibre, but also removes much of the food's value too, including B vitamins, healthy oils and fat-soluble vitamins. These carbs are then digested very quickly, giving an energy spike which is usually followed by a steep dip and hunger.

Blood sugar: Anytime we eat a carbohydrate, our bodies convert it into glucose and send this glucose to our blood. Glucose is just the name given to sugar once it is in the blood. Blood sugars rise and fall each day, and the steadier these changes are the better. As you may have guessed already, sugary foods cause spikes in blood sugar levels, which temporarily make us feel good and energized. This may sound like a good idea, but the issue is that this isn't the case for long – low mood and fatigue quickly follow. The aim of the game is to keep these levels steady as much as we can.

What about potatoes?

Although potatoes are not refined in the same way that the other dumb carbs are, they have a lower nutrient value than their root vegetable cousins, partly due to cultivation modifications over the years, which have sought to make them bigger, rounder and fluffier (the consequence being that they are more starchy and therefore have more sugar). Swapping them for sweet potatoes, smaller new potatoes or other starchy veggies like parsnips is a great upgrade.

Unless, like revenge, they are served cold!   An interesting fact about cold potatoes: the simple act of cooling turns them into a super food for your gut. The same applies for rice and pasta too. As they cool, they change the starch molecules to resistant starch, which is why cold potatoes feel firmer. That this starch is resistant means that it's resistant to digestion, so it just acts as a filler, making you feel full up and lowering the sugar hit that you would expect from a carb, as it is no longer absorbable to the body. It also provides food (pre-biotics) for the good bacteria in our guts (see page 56), which feed, thrive and proliferate on resistant starch. Potato salad is well and truly back on the menu!

What about our daily bread then?

After 30,000 years of bread being present in the human diet, has society been rightly influenced by this no/less bread movement?

Perhaps bread is not the demon it has been made out to be, and can be a regular feature in a healthy, balanced Work Fuel diet. We are referring here to good-quality, sourdough (if possible), wholegrain, additive-free bread, *not* the processed stuff that lasts on the shelf for three months and needs a scientist to translate the ingredients lists.

For a quick check to see if your bread ticks the right boxes, take the grams of carbohydrate from the nutritional information on the label and divide it by the grams of fibre (you'll see the formula below). A good carbohydrate to fibre ratio is less than ten. This is a simple way to weed out the sugary excuses for bread! If it doesn't have a label, like in an actual bakery, it's generally likely to be of better quality. If you're not sure what to choose, go for dark sourdough bread that has some weight to it.

$$\frac{\text{GRAMS OF CARBOHYDRATE}}{\text{GRAMS OF FIBRE}}$$

SMARTER BREAD
= less than **10**

• **REMEMBER THIS** •

Freezing bread turns some of the easily digested starch it contains into resistant starch, lowering the blood sugar response to the carbs in the bread.[22] Just like the cooling of the potato. This benefit is not lost once the bread has been defrosted.

Upgrade your concentration, switch to smarter carbs

Switching these out in the kitchen means you just naturally default to an upgraded fuel, without having to think about it. Graham loved pasta when he first started working with Colette, and as it was a regular feature in his life, we just swapped the regular stuff for black bean pasta right at the start – an easy fix without too much of a shift required.

Here are some easy smarter-carb swaps to make – and the flavour gets upgraded too:

Ditch	Switch
Cream cracker	Oatcake
Crisps	Popcorn (home-popped is best)
White, fluffy potatoes	Sweet potato, parsnips, swedes
Commercial cereals	Oat and chia seed porridge
White rice	Brown rice
White bread	Sourdough/wholewheat/rye bread
White pasta	Black bean/wholewheat/spelt pasta
Couscous	Quinoa/lentils/beans/legumes/barley

● REMEMBER THIS ●

When changing your diet, it's important to do it gradually, as your body takes time to adjust. If you don't eat vegetables regularly, then moving to ten a day straight away is likely to cause some digestive discomfort, shall we say. Your gut bacteria need to catch up and there may be a period of adjustment that is a little uncomfortable while this happens; your body is recalibrating. So, if you do make some changes, and get some 'feedback', dial it back a little, but stick it out.

SUPPLEMENTARY INGREDIENT NO. 1: FAT

How much? Use oils/fats like you would a condiment: a tablespoon is a rough serving.

The brain is 60% fat (once we remove the water, that is). Yet most of us have been duped by the low-fat bandwagon, leaving our brains starved of its favourite nutrient. A low-fat diet not only makes us less intelligent (really), it is also not the quick fix to a fat-free body that many hope it is.[23]

Luckily, we are seeing a new wave of change when it comes to fat – positive headlines, books and even TV programmes on the 'eat the fat' bandwagon, and the *British Medical Journal* (*BMJ*) has published a landmark paper entitled 'Saturated fat does not clog the arteries'.[24] This has been pivotal in leading the charge and we are seeing a paradigm shift in the doctor's surgery too. This is good news for our precious brains, as without it we are literally starving the most crucial organ of the body of its crucial fuel and zapping our productivity.[25]

Eating naturally full-fat options will result in more satiety, more complete nutrition, better absorption of some nutrients, fewer hidden nasties and fewer cravings. Hence, full-fat foods are better for your energy and focus than low-fat ones with their own jingles. They also taste so much better. No more low-fat, tasteless options – hurray!

There is a fat to ditch

Having said all that, there is one category of fats that should be avoided: trans unsaturated fats (trans fats). These are found in processed foods and are made from plant oils that are heated to high temperatures and hydrogenated. They give food long shelf lives, add a rich, buttery flavour and are super-cheap. Items such as margarine, snack foods in general like crisps, cereal bars, mass-made dips and baked packaged goods, like breads, pastries, cakes and wraps, are all likely to contain trans fats.

These foods are productivity and intelligence killers. A study in 2015 found that for every additional gram of trans fat a participant ate, their word recall dropped. This was found to be particularly relevant in adults under 45 years of age. The biscuits you grabbed at the first meeting this morning for a 'bit of a boost' don't seem like such a good idea any more.[26] Trans fats are killing us off earlier too – the *BMJ* reported in 2015 that their consumption was associated with a 34% increased risk of death. They have called for a careful review of dietary guidelines for these nutrients.[27]

Immediate action for your fridge and kitchen cupboards:

▶ **DITCH** vegetable oils or oils from seeds: rapeseed, soybean, corn, sunflower and safflower. Unlike coconut or olive oil that can be extracted by pressing, the totally unnatural processing of these oils creates trans fats. There is a case for some of these, like rapeseed, to remain, if cold-pressed and extra virgin.

▶ **SWITCH** to butter, coconut oil and extra virgin olive oil.

Turn down the temperature when using any oil. As soon as the oil starts to smoke it begins to become less nutriful and more toxic. Cooking at less than 200 degrees Celsius (392 degrees Fahrenheit) is better for keeping the nutrition and taste in, and the burnt flavour out.

▶ **DITCH** margarine forever please.

▶ **DITCH** processed foods that are likely to contain trans fats – pastries, biscuits, commercial breads, ready meals and vegan spreads.

More on this in the kitchen detox, in Chapter 8, but this point is so important we do not want you to have to wait until then.

The Wonder Oil – Extra Virgin Olive Oil (EVOO)

EVOO deserves a special mention. Central to the Mediterranean diet, there have been countless studies on the effects of this oil that is more like a medicine. It has been shown in a large long-term study to protect the brain against decline and even improve cognitive function. In one study, which lasted for six and a half years, some of the groups were consuming a litre per week! And they saw no weight gain or negative side effects. In fact, EVOO was shown to block an enzyme in fatty tissue called fatty acid synthase, which creates fat from excess carbs. Crazy, since so many people still believe the low-fat hype.[28]

EVOO should be the main oil in your diet, used on salads, as a marinade, drizzled over roasting veggies and to add flavour to soups.

What about a bigger brain?

Add a daily dose of essential fatty acids (EFAs). These are essential as they can't be made within the human body, and therefore their benefits can only be gained through eating them. They come in a couple of sizes: omega-6 and our beloved brain-boosting omega-3.

Omega-3 is associated with increased brain performance and executive function, affecting our decision-making, self-control and attention. Evidence from numerous studies has shown that the more omega-3 a population eats, the lower the incidence of mental health issues they experience.

Omega-6s are pro-inflammatory, meaning that they are capable of causing inflammation. This is a necessary process of the immune system; it is part of the body's healing process. Without it we wouldn't be able to respond to injury or infection. Omega-6's promoting of the inflammatory response is essential to halt cell damage and promote cell repair. However, the issues arise when the amounts of these fats that we consume are out of balance.

It is understood that the body evolved on a ratio of 1:1 of these fats.[29] Yet we have totally skewed this ratio, with some reports claiming that the ratio we consume is 20:1 and higher in favour of omega-6. These oils are now so plentiful in our diets that we are rarely, if ever, deficient, yet a distorted ratio of these fatty acids may be one of the most damaging aspects of the Western diet.[30]

To even out the odds, we need to reduce the omega-6s and eat more omega-3. The richest dietary source of omega-3s is from oily fish, so eating this two to three times per week will help.

● **REMEMBER THIS** ●

Fish is the most effective way to top up our brains with this fat, as it contains eicosapentaenoic acid (EPA) and docosahexaenoic acid (DHA), the most important omega-3 fats. We have lightning-speed thinking and thought processes when these are topped up regularly! If you are not a fish eater, you can supplement. In a study at Berlin's Charité Hospital, adults were given a supplement containing 1,320 mg of EPA and 880 mg DHA, roughly equivalent to a 100 g serving of salmon. Their executive function was enhanced by 26% compared to the placebo group.[31]

Can you imagine 26% extra decision-making power? Twenty-six per cent more attention? Or 26% additional self-control?

You can also get omega-3 from plants: walnuts; flaxseed; pumpkin, hemp and chia seeds; dark green veggies and some seaweeds. If this is your only source of omega-3 you have to eat these foods most days or add in a supplement, as omega-3 from plant sources isn't as absorbable for the body as it is from fish, and the DHA and EPA are in lower quantities.

Omega-6 oils are found in the same sources as the trans fats we mentioned above, and in some of the ditch list and in fatty animal products like bacon. They are also found in more natural sources like nuts and seeds, but in much lower and less worrying amounts.

Walnuts deserve a special mention, as they even look like a little brain – perhaps it's nature's way of telling us of their potential power! Each walnut is made up of around 65% fat, particularly the good omega-3 fat, and 20% protein. Walnuts are also rich in the antioxidant vitamin E, which helps to fight against free-radical damage in the brain and may reduce the risk of neurodegenerative diseases such as Alzheimer's.[32] They also contain vitamin B6 to promote healthy serotonin levels in the brain.

Not everyone can digest nuts comfortably; this may be due in part to the phytic acid on the outside. Nutrition purists would insist that you soak all nuts before eating to remove this acid. It is worth doing this, especially if you currently don't eat these nutrition powerhouses due to this reason. They just need to be submerged in water with a teaspoon of salt for around six hours, rinsed and then they are ready to eat. Store in the fridge once they have been soaked, and eat within a day or two.

Opt for naturally full-fat options
Seek out the beneficial fats and add some to each meal – foods such as avocado, nuts, seeds and even butter and full-fat yoghurt. By the way, full-fat milk and yoghurt products are anything but 'full of fat' – they are 96% fat free! Yes, it's true. They contain (naturally) only around 4% fat, meaning they only just miss out on the classification of 'low-fat', which is 3%. A 2013 review published in the *European Journal of Nutrition* found that people who eat full-fat dairy tend to be leaner than those who opt for low-fat versions[33] – probably because these products tend to contain more protein, and less sugar too.

It's crazy to think that for many people, 'fat' has for a long time either been something to avoid, or something that can only be consumed in heavily processed products. In Colette's workshops across the world this remains evident, with many still avoiding eggs based on out-of-date headlines while cooking with vegetable oils and spreading margarine on otherwise healthy foods, as the marketing on these products has convinced them it's the 'healthy' option. Spread the word – you'll feel a whole lot better for eating the healthy fats again.

SUPPLEMENTARY INGREDIENT NO. 2: FERMENTED FOODS

How much? Use fermented foods like you would a condiment – to top a dish with.

Eat foods that have been cultured to contain healthy bacteria. You may not have ever linked the health of your gut to your productivity, but we are here to tell you that there is most definitely a link and there are a couple of actions you may be overlooking each day that can massively upgrade its function. Some of these upgrades can take effect in just one day!

In the last few years there has been huge interest in our gut, specifically the bacteria (over a trillion types of microorganisms), by neuroscientists. Researchers have begun to understand the influence of our gut microbiome, the bacteria that live symbiotically within our digestive system, and how it effects our cognition and emotions. There is a two-way communication system between the central nervous system and the gut, known as the enteric nervous system. It's literally like another brain. In fact, the gut tells the brain more than the brain tells the gut. Your gut changes your emotional state and other related brain systems, and your brain changes your gut. Ever experienced butterflies in your stomach in response to stress? Or had to run to the loo when anxious about a presentation?

Cultivate your 'home' fans to set yourself up for more wins
You may not be a football fan, but it's well known that each team has its own ground, a stadium where they are based and where they play their home games. Let's take the Theatre of Dreams, Manchester United's Old Trafford stadium (mainly because Colette was writing this bit and she wouldn't let Graham have the Aston Villa stadium). This has capacity for 74,994 people, yet only 3,000 of this capacity is set aside each game for 'away' fans. The Manchester United management want to create an environment where their team is most likely to win, and by filling the ground with their fans, all rooting for the team's success, they are more likely to. Makes sense, right?

Well, our guts are like our very own football stadium. The more we can fill it with home fans – that is, friendly gut bacteria, encouraging us to succeed – the more successful we are likely to be. The home fans like to receive properly chewed, colourful, fibre-rich, varied foods, with fermented options thrown in each day too. This keeps them thriving and cheering us on, willing us to succeed.

The problems begin when we let too many away fans in. These guys gain entrance via processed, repetitive foods. They love sugar, caffeine and alcohol too. Once they are in, they rain on the parade of the home bacteria, they crowd them out and start to run the ground. While they're booing and jeering from the sidelines, we start to feel low and bloated and our energy and confidence take a hit. We get sick and we just don't have the same verve as before. This is known medically as gut dysbiosis. Basically our gut family is out of balance. Imagine this at a game – how successful do you think that team would be if this played out week after week?

What are fermented foods?

Fermenting means getting bacteria to pre-digest food for us, making it easier for us to digest and more nutritious, and leaving some bacterial friends to populate our guts with. So much to like! Here are some suggestions to include on your plate:

1. **Sauerkraut.** Made from just cabbage and salt, you can use it to top salads, stuff in sandwiches or even as garnish for warm dishes too.

2. **Kimchi.** This is sauerkraut's spicy Korean twin. It can be used in a similar way, and is also great on egg dishes.

3. **Miso.** A fermented paste made from barley, rice or soybeans, miso adds a nice rich flavour to dishes. It's bold, so a little goes a long way. Usually used in soups, but also makes salad dressings and marinades even more delicious and gut healthy.

4. **Tempeh.** Made from naturally fermented soybeans, it has a firm texture and a slightly nutty flavour.

5. **Yoghurt.** Yoghurt is made by fermenting milk (dairy-free options count too). Just check it says 'live' on the label and then buy the unsweetened and unflavoured varieties.

6. **Kombucha.** Made from fermented black or green tea, it's a tangy, fizzy drink that's rich in bacteria. You can buy flavoured varieties too – just check the sugar content (22.5 g of total sugars or more is high, 5 g of total sugars or less is low).

7. **Kefir.** A fermented milk drink, it tastes like drinkable yoghurt. It's delicious as a base in smoothies. Buy the unsweetened and unflavoured varieties.

As we are now living in an increasingly sterile world, eating more fermented foods is the intelligent way to go. Eating these foods most days as part of your regular diet will optimize your intestinal flora, boosting your immune system, mental health, energy and digestive absorption rates.[34] They are tasty too. To ensure you are getting the real deal, check the label for added sugars, vinegar and other additives. There shouldn't be more than two ingredients in sauerkraut, for example: cabbage and salt. Oh, and if it says pasteurized then our bacterial buddies will have been wiped out, so look out for this.

A diverse gut is a happy gut
When we eat a diverse diet, we are more likely to receive a whole spectrum of nutrients, which means that deficiencies are less likely. Our gut bacteria love dietary diversity as they get fed by the different nutrients and thrive; we then get happier, less anxious and more mentally clear.[35]

However, 50 crops now deliver 90% of the world's calories.[36] It's little more than half a century since several thousand plants would have done the same. How did we become so boring? According to Bioversity International, an international research and policy organization, just three crops – rice, wheat and corn, provide more than half of plant-derived calories consumed worldwide.[37]

The good news is there are still things that we can do to ensure that we get a variety of nutrients. We have already spoken about eating the rainbow. This act alone will ensure that we are increasing the diversity of our diet. But to be a little more prescriptive and to measure your success, we have a challenge for you that your gut bacteria will love.

Eat 30 – the food diversity challenge

According to the American Gut Study, our gut bacteria thrive when we eat around 30 different, brightly coloured plant foods per week.[38] Initially this was just a hypothesis, now it's science. To encourage and measure dietary diversity, try the following exercise. You may find it helpful to download the 'Eat 30 Food Challenge' template from **www.workfuel.ninja/eat30**

EXERCISE: EAT 30 CHALLENGE

Time:
3–5 mins after each meal

What you'll need:
Pen and chart below

Ninja mindset:
Unorthodoxy, Agility

In one week eat 30 different plant foods: how diverse and interesting can you be? A varied diet that is loaded with rainbow-coloured foods helps keep our guts happy. A happy gut = a happy brain and well-functioning body.

What counts? All plant foods: vegetables, fruit, fresh herbs, nuts and seeds. If you're worried about the cost, remember that not everything needs to be fresh – you can buy many of these foods frozen, tinned and in bulk. Keep track of each plant food you eat for a week:

1.	7.	13.	19.	25.
2.	8.	14. Halfway, the home fans are cheering…	20.	26.
3.	9.	15.	21.	27.
4.	10.	16.	22.	28.
5.	11.	17.	23.	29.
6. Great streak, keep it up	12.	18.	24.	30. A packed out stadium, League winners!

SUPPLEMENTARY INGREDIENT NO. 3: HYDRATION

How much? As a guide, eight glasses or one and a half to two litres per day (but it depends, see below).

Water doesn't appear on most food charts, but it is critical to brain function, so we believe it deserves to be alongside the Work Fuel Plate. Around 75% of the brain is water, so dehydration can seriously affect cognitive functions such as memory, reasoning, attention span, concentration, mood and decision-making. When the brain is dehydrated, you're also more likely to feel tired and experience headaches. In a study by Cambridge University, conducted on young men, where the experimenters induced just 1% dehydration, they found that this stimulated adverse changes in vigilance and working memory, and increased tension/anxiety and fatigue.[39]

In another study, for the *Journal of Nutrition*, when subjects experienced only minor dehydration (only 1.36% of their body mass) they were more likely to suffer from frequent headaches, lapses of concentration and unusual bouts of tiredness than those with no dehydration.[40]

Even minimal dehydration can affect our physical health and cognitive functioning, hampering productivity. While we've noticed a shift in recent years in many of our clients' offices, it's still easy for many of us to go hours without drinking water at our desks, or at best it's coffee or tea. Often the room is air conditioned, which increases dehydration.

Water is vital. In fact, Colette has seen a whole host of complaints clear up through proper hydration, like headaches, low energy, difficulty concentrating, and even bags under the eyes have vanished.

The gold standard for hydration is water, perhaps adding in a slice of lemon or lime, cucumber or a few mint leaves, or even a pinch of Himalayan rock salt (this mineralizes the water, adding some electrolytes, and so makes it even more hydrating, especially after physical activity). As a guideline, you have probably heard the eight glasses per day advice. While we couldn't find an actual study to underpin this, as a guide it seems to work. If it's hot or you're in an air-conditioned environment, presenting all day, exercising and so on, you may need more.

The best way to know how much you personally need? Go and look at your own wee. You're aiming for a colour that is light yellow. Too much and it will be clear – you can step off your intake if it is. Too dark and you need to drink more. Check out our chart at **www.workfuel.ninja/takingthepee**

Are you eating when you should be drinking?
We've all heard it at some point – if you're hungry and it's not lunch/dinner time, drink a glass of water. It is worth repeating. Often, thirst is mistaken for hunger and in fact, you are simply dehydrated and thirsty. Having a drink and allowing ten to fifteen minutes for the body to register it is a simple way to establish if this is in fact the case.

Be a camel: carry it
We can't assume that hydration is always going to be provided, so like a camel in the desert, carry it for yourself. Invest in a glass or metal water bottle, fill it up a few times a day and problem solved. If you can filter your tap water, then all the better. Most plastic bottles contain bisphenol A (BPA). This is a known sex-hormone disruptor, as it mimics oestrogen in the body and it has been linked to endocrine disorders, such as fertility issues and male impotence.[41] It's expensive for the planet as well as your wallet, so please ditch plastic water bottles and carry a reusable one instead.

What about tap water?
Tap water, albeit certified 'safe' to drink, has been through miles of pipelines, picking up contaminants along the way. It has been disinfected with things like chlorine that not only make it smell and taste a bit funny, but are also chemicals we could do with a bit less of. We know it may seem a faff, but if you can, choose a jug or bottle with a filter, which will remove some of the contaminants, but will allow the minerals that we need to remain. There are some more expensive installed options for the home, so you don't have to bother with the filtering at all. A popular myth is that bottled water is better than tap water, but this isn't always true – sometimes it may have come from the tap anyhow.[42]

Don't drink food*
Drinking bypasses lots of our natural food control system. Just think how easy it is to drink a large glass of apple juice, yet you wouldn't sit down and eat eight apples in one sitting – after the second one the control system would step in and say you have had enough. The whole apple contains fibre, which slows the release of the apple's sugar and in doing so balances the effect of eating it on our energy. Without the fibre it sends us on a rollercoaster of energy cycles, starting with a boost and ending in a crash. The crash may be just at the point when you are asked to stand up and present your ideas or you need to kick off that complex task on your to-do list. It's just not worth it. Sugary caffeine drinks have a similar if not more profound effect, yet large coffee shop chains take great delight in selling us expensive, iced or cream-topped drinks that are equivalent to an extra meal, but will simply not register as one – starting a blood sugar crash cycle all over again.

---

* Unless it's a Work Fuel smoothie, that is (see Chapter 3), which, by the way, we recommend you chew.

EXERCISE: THE WORK FUEL PLATE – HOW DO YOU MEASURE UP?

Time:
5–10 minutes

What you'll need:
Pen and paper (or write in the book)
plus good memory recall!

Ninja mindset:
Mindfulness

Step 1: Write down the last three meals you ate:

Meal 1: ....

....

....

Meal 2: ....

....

....

Meal 3: ....

....

....

Step 2: Fill in the empty plates below with the percentages of the meal, just approximate – rainbow plants percentage, protein percentage, smarter carbs percentage, and make a note of any fermented foods, fats or oils:

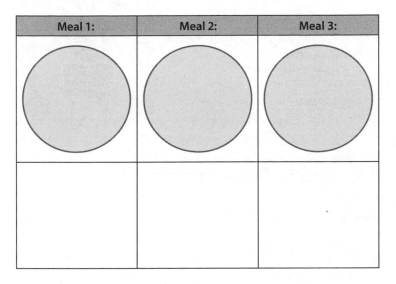

Meal 1:	Meal 2:	Meal 3:

Step 3: Compare them to the Work Fuel Plate. How did you measure up? Where's the biggest gap? Write this down. This is a clue as to where to start. How can you upgrade your next meal?

Are you a Ninja?

► A Ninja adopts a 'plant slant' to their food, using the Work Fuel Plate as a guide to get the right levels of rainbow plants, smarter carbs and protein, as well as focusing on good fats such as omega-3 and fermented foods.

► A Ninja knows that water is as vital to brain function as food – and prepares by keeping a water bottle in their bag or a filter jug on their desk.

► A Ninja also knows that gut bacteria play a vital role in digestion and energy and eats a wide range of plant foods to cultivate good gut health.

3.
BREAKFAST

BREAK THE FAST, EAT SLOW

If you start strong, you set the tone for the entire day. If you start weak, the opposite is also most definitely true. View this meal as breaking the fast (break-fast), but also try to think about

'Breakfast isn't the most important meal of the day, but it may just be the most important choice of the day.'
– Aubrey Marcus

breaking the habit of having a fast breakfast, in two senses. Firstly, ditch the fast-metabolizing breakfast foods, like sugary cereals and refined white breads and pastries (dumb carbs). Secondly, start making time to take breakfast, even if it's just fifteen minutes, rather than grabbing something on the go, while jumping onto a train and updating a social media feed at the same time.

WHO HAS TIME FOR BREAKFAST?

Successful people have time for breakfast. When our body and brain are starved, we can start to feel low in energy, foggy and more easily overwhelmed, contributing to overall feelings of stress. Our brains need glucose to survive, and when you skip a meal and your body goes into starvation mode, your cognitive functions, along with attention and memory, take a nosedive.

The neurotransmitters that impact our mood are affected when meals are skipped, so eating breakfast leads you to feel more in control and less overwhelmed in relation to tasks at hand. It sets you up for a more energized, productive day ahead. Your metabolism and blood sugar control are also better in the morning than they are later in the day, so it makes good sense to eat more food earlier on.

WHAT ABOUT ALL THE TRENDY PEOPLE SKIPPING BREAKFAST?

Well, if you're in a hotel and all you have on offer is sugary options, like crumpets, muffins, pastries and commercial cereals, then an option is to skip breakfast altogether and fast until lunch. A sugar-centric breakfast like this is going to sabotage any productivity efforts before the day has even started.

However, most of the time there is a better way. Check the labels, ask for an egg, some fresh fruit or yoghurt. We've got more information on what to do in these sorts of situations in Chapter 7.

In recent times, fasting has become a rapidly growing trend and skipping breakfast in many of the protocols is part of it. While there is lots of advice out there, the science remains unclear and conflicted. It's generally still agreed that breakfast is important. However, we'll talk a bit more about other types of fasting in Chapter 5.

If you are the kind of person who is just not hungry in the morning, perhaps this is due to habit, rather than what your body needs. Start small, maybe a handful of nuts or a scoop of Greek yoghurt topped with berries. Give it a few weeks and if you still feel sick at the thought of it, then maybe this one isn't for you and lunch needs to take even more of a priority. We shouldn't be eating if we are not hungry. It's worth a try though, as gaining more energy is the likely payback. Give it a chance to take effect, as it may take a while to retrain your stomach.

WHAT ABOUT MY MORNING COFFEE(S)?

Let's hone in here on caffeine. The most potent source tends to be coffee, but it's also contained in smaller amounts in green and black tea, and chocolate. Not forgetting fizzy and energy drinks too, although the latter should not feature in your working day at all, more of which later on.

You will have heard about the damaging effects of coffee and caffeine on our bodies: the jitters, anxiety, mood swings, blood sugar imbalances, dehydration, and the fact that it recreates stress conditions on the body which, repeated too often, can lead to burnout.[1] This may be all true, but we are not into demonizing a real food. Instead we would prefer some context – if you are experiencing anxiety or feel stressed, for example, then you are wise to totally avoid caffeinated products. It's worth noting that there is a lot of individual variability when it comes to tolerance for caffeine; for some people one cup of coffee is enough to experience negative side effects.

Decision or dependency?
We generally drink coffee (or caffeinated drinks like tea) for two main reasons – we like the taste or we need it to mask tiredness. If it's the latter and this is a daily occurrence then this is now no longer a decision, it's dependency. Ask yourself, why are you so chronically tired? Is it lack of good-quality sleep, eating habits, taking too much on, or is it a regular feeling of caffeine lull? Whatever it is, overriding your own tiredness for a long time leads to only one thing: burnout.

So, what can you do, if you can relate to this? Firstly, drink a glass of water with each coffee or caffeinated drink. This will buffer the side effects to some extent, at the very least ensuring you are not as dehydrated when drinking coffee, as this for sure will mean jitter time – something that we see daily in the workplace.

Next, look to gradually reduce your consumption, swapping it out for perhaps black or green tea in the short term. They both contain caffeine, so you are still getting a lift, but a milder one as the levels are lower and their compounds affect us in a more gentle manner. We don't recommend going cold turkey, as it can be painful dependent on your current levels of caffeine intake – headache, muscle ache, irritability … Not nice.

Coffee as brain fuel

Coffee is actually one of the most nutrient-dense foods on the planet, packed full of plant chemicals that have lots of beneficial effects on our bodies: they reduce inflammation, can help control blood sugar levels and promote antioxidant activity, which equals lots of productivity gains, not to mention lower risk of stroke, Alzheimer's and heart attack.[2]

The trick is to consume caffeine in moderation. Try to limit your caffeine intake to 300 mg per day from all sources – coffee, tea and dark chocolate. One medium cup of coffee contains around 100 mg of caffeine, a cup of green tea around 40 mg.

Fizzy and energy drinks?

Never drink energy drinks or fizzy drinks thinking they're brain fuel. They will give you the *feeling* of fuel, usually via a caffeine or blood sugar spike, but that's all. They contain a cocktail of additives, ranging from high-fructose corn syrups, or chemical sweeteners if they are no/low sugar, to colourings and preservatives. Check out Chapter 6 for more on these. Some of these drinks are so bad, they come with health warnings. The UK's NHS issued a special warning about energy drinks, highlighting detrimental effects on dental health, and a link to miscarriage and even how they contribute to death![3] They don't sound like a treat to us. If you're particularly keen on the fizz, we'd suggest using sparkling or soda water, jazzed up with a slice of lime or lemon.

Cut it out after noon

Whether you are a big caffeine drinker or not, the best advice is to cut it out from noon onwards. Caffeine is a big sleep disruptor. Adenosine is a chemical that builds up in the body the longer we are awake. The more we have, the sleepier we feel. Caffeine blocks adenosine receptors, fooling the body into thinking it is not tired when it comes to bedtime – enter the feeling of being 'wired and tired'. Caffeine has around a six-hour half-life (the time it takes for the caffeine concentration in our blood to be reduced by half), which means it sticks around in our bloodstreams for a while, and anything after lunchtime is going to have the potential to disrupt our sleep. This can vary from person to person and can last for as long as ten hours in some people. Also, our tolerance levels can change, so maybe once you could tolerate much more than you can now. With this simple act of no caffeine after noon, heaps of Colette's clients have seen massive improvements in their quality of sleep in a short period of time.

> ● **REMEMBER THIS** ●
>
> *Opt for a light roast* Research shows that longer roasting robs coffee of an important chemical, chlorogenic acid. This acid can help regulate our energy, through improving blood sugar management, but roasting destroys most of this healthful compound. The darker the coffee bean, the less chlorogenic acid it has. So, opt for a lighter roast and you get more of the good stuff.[4]

What about decaf?

Firstly, decaffeinated does not mean no caffeine, it means lower caffeine. Usually around 90% of the caffeine is removed, but this can vary dependent on the brand and how it is prepared. Also, the caffeine-removal process varies between brands and in some cases questionable chemicals are used that may leave a residue behind. The science seems to be inconclusive on the effects of this residue, but there is sound research saying that you can get similar health benefits as from regular coffee, minus the buzz, from decaf, without the negative side effects of caffeine.[5] So, for the caffeine-sensitive and as a gateway to reduce caffeine dependence, decaf is a good way to go.

Upgrade to vitality

Start the day with water, not caffeine. Swap out your first coffee for a plain glass of water, maybe even warm and with a squeeze of lemon if you want to be cooking on gas for the rest of the day! This simple act sets your energy dial at max. We wake dehydrated, our bodies craving a drink – and then most

people's first drink of the day is caffeine, which is a diuretic. It literally removes more water from the body, leaving you low on energy and setting you up for a cycle of yo-yoing all day.

The temperature of the water we drink does make a difference too: drinking room-temperature water aids digestion, promotes detox and speeds up hydration. When you drink cold water, your blood vessels shrink, and this restricts your digestion. Warm water helps break down food, reduces constipation, and even helps you lose weight while improving your blood circulation.

WHAT SHOULD I EAT FOR BREAKFAST?

Within each of the meal chapters (Chapters 3–5) we will give you at least five example meals that are aligned to the Work Fuel Plate and the Work Fuel Way, aiming to give you a balanced amount of protein, carbohydrates, fats and nutrients. Breakfast is usually the place we miss out the protein and fats and eat more carbohydrates – this is your chance to correct that and fuel in a more appropriate way. In addition, there will be a single recipe that you can make once and eat for a week, with a varied topping of your choice. At breakfast it may be a little harder to include vegetables, as we automatically opt for fruit at this time of the day. This may be where you eat your fruit for the day, but experiment with a few extra vegetables anywhere you can. Remember the Work Fuel essential consistency over intensity here – a one-hour luxurious healthy breakfast on Monday will not cut it all week. On the other hand, investing fifteen minutes for

a breakfast each day that's packed with the choices described here on four days out of five days will. Same time, better return.

Here are a couple of Work Fuel breakfast superstars, which have been on the morning menu for years:

Oats

Start your day with healthy slow-burning carbohydrates. Oats contain sugars that are released slowly into the bloodstream for sustained energy release, and as a result they are a great source of long-lasting morning energy. In contrast, sugary cereals cause sudden spikes in energy, followed by a crash in blood sugar levels. Oats fuel the brain and satisfy hunger, reducing the chance of a midday crash.

Oats also contain choline, which is needed for the body to produce an important neurotransmitter for memory called acetylcholine.[6] There is a huge variety of oat products available, which vary widely in quality. Opt for the bigger flakes – they are less processed than other oats, and top with other brain-boosting foods such as blueberries and walnuts.

Beans

Beans are packed with smarter carbohydrates, fibre, vitamins, minerals and protein. The combination of their complex carbs and fibre provides a slow and steady release of energy throughout the day. Beans are also rich in iron, low levels of which can result in low mood, irritability, confusion and other cognitive issues. Beans are an excellent source of folate (the natural form of folic acid) and vitamin B6, both of which are important to our cognition, mood and brain ageing.[7] Unfortunately the classic baked beans are bathed in refined sugar and salts. Think black beans, kidney beans and butter beans instead. Still a fan of baked beans? Then create your own – recipe page 219.

Upgrade the classics

The great thing about the Work Fuel Way is that you don't have to totally transform your lifestyle to see big results. Simply upgrading what you do already can go a long way. Here are a few ideas for upgrades at breakfast time:

Classic	Upgrade
Cheese on toast	Smarter bread, unprocessed cheese (be label-savvy: just a couple of ingredients is what we're looking for – maybe even fermented too) and topped with mushrooms, tomatoes and onion.
Pancakes	Swap out the flour for a banana (1 banana:1 egg) and mix/blend the batter as per usual.
Beans on toast	Smarter bread, make your own beans as per recipe on page 219 or buy the low-sugar variety and add extras.
Full English	Grill it, smarter bread and 50% vegetables – mushrooms, tomatoes, beans, spinach, avocado.

The following recipes can be adapted for vegetarians and vegans and there are tasty options to make the night before, as well as items you can take with you on the go. They all take less than fifteen minutes, some just two minutes. No excuses.

1. Toast

Smart bread choice, one or two slices – top it and mix them up

Time 5–10 minutes

- ▶ 1–3 eggs any way you like (boiled, poached, fried, scrambled), add a mix of veggies – tomato, cucumber, spinach – black pepper, paprika
- ▶ Cottage cheese, soft-boiled egg, spring onions, tomatoes, red pepper and paprika
- ▶ Avocado, spinach, cottage cheese and spicy kimchee
- ▶ Nut butter, banana, berries and cinnamon
- ▶ Greek or plant yoghurt, banana, blueberries, chia seeds and cinnamon
- ▶ Buffalo mozzarella, cherry tomatoes, spinach and fresh basil.

2. Work Fuel Smoothie Formula

Visualize the ingredients on the Work Fuel Plate before they are blended

Time 5 minutes

See the table overleaf.

Optional **brain enhancers** to add to the list overleaf are:

- ▶ Fresh (1 tbsp): ginger, turmeric or herbs of choice
- ▶ Dried (1 tsp): ginger, cinnamon, cacao, açai powder, turmeric.

Create your own blend by mixing up the ingredients. Always ensure you have covered steps one to three. Share your #workfuelsmoothie experiments with us on social media.

Top tip: double the ingredients and make enough for two meals. Store in the fridge for a maximum of 24 hours, adding a squeeze of lemon juice to help to preserve it.

Step 1	Step 2	Step 3	Step 4	Step 5
Choose your base – 1 cup of water then add in a further 1–2 cups of an option below	Choose a protein – 1–2 tbsp	Choose your greens – 1–2 cups	Choose a fruit or sweet vegetable – ½ cup or 1 piece	Choose a fat – 1–2 tbsp
• Water • Vegetable juice (100%) • Herbal tea (ginger, cinnamon, peppermint) • Nut milk • Coconut water • Milk	• Chia seeds • Hemp seeds • Nut butter • Greek yoghurt • Kefir • Protein powder	• Spinach • Kale • Romaine lettuce • Celery • Cucumber • Parsley	• Berries • Apple • Carrot • Beetroot • Peach • Pear	• Avocado • Nuts • Hemp seeds • Coconut oil • Coconut • Tahini • Nut butter (including peanut butter)

3. Work Fuel Porridge, three ways
Time 5–10 minutes

The Work Fuel Porridge base is an upgrade on the usual. It is a blend of porridge oats (6 level tbsp) and chia seeds or ground flaxseed (2 tbsp) for extra protein and omega-3. The ratio is 3:1, so if you need a little less or a little more of the finished porridge, adjust accordingly.

▶ **The classic.** Add the porridge base and 350 ml/1 mug water or milk of your choice to a saucepan. You can try more or less water or milk if you like it thinner or thicker. It will thicken on standing. Bring it to the boil and simmer for 4–5 minutes, stirring from time to time and watching carefully that it doesn't stick to the bottom of the pan.

Top it with your choice of apple, berries, kiwi, nuts, seeds, cacao, kefir, yoghurt and plenty of cinnamon. Porridge lends itself very well to customization, so you can adapt it to suit your palate and vary it when you want something new.

▶ **The fashionable.** Overnight oats (code for cold porridge – it doesn't really have the same ring to it!). Add the porridge base and liquid together as described in the classic recipe above, but leave out the heat. Prepare it in a jar for a quick exit or make once in a big sealed container and eat it for days. The oats soak up the milk overnight and like a mini-miracle you wake up to creamy, oaty goodness. This is a social media star, check #overnightoats for further inspiration.

▶ **The savoury.** Who said porridge has to be sweet? We have a great savoury recipe to share (page 218). It encourages veggies at brekkie and you can batch it too.

4. Yoghurt

Think Greek! Natural Greek yoghurt is a strained yoghurt, which means that the protein is more concentrated, making it a good, satisfying choice at breakfast; if you can't track it down, opt for live natural yoghurt and top with stewed or chopped fruit, nuts and seeds. Another option is plant yoghurts, like unflavoured varieties of coconut or a vegan kefir, to get your good bacteria dose earlier in the day.

> ● **REMEMBER THIS** ●
>
> Sprinkle your yoghurt (or any dish you like) with cinnamon. Research shows it can improve the body's ability to regulate blood sugar and this aromatic spice also boosts brain activity, by stimulating the birth of new neurons in the brain and encouraging the survival of existing neurons.[8]

5. Cook once, eat for a week – breakfast beans

This is a great dish if you know you are going to be busy all week. It packs a veggie punch and is cheap and easy to prepare. It can be eaten hot or cold, with an egg on top, with grated cheese or with a slice of toast. You can double or triple the quantities and freeze. The recipe is on page 219, just try it.

Finally, I am walking out the door and I don't have any time, I haven't prepped anything …

No plate or glass required:

▶ Half an avocado with lime, salt and chilli

▶ Piece of fruit with a handful of nuts

▶ Fruit (sliceable) of choice, e.g. apple, topped with nut butter (peanut, cashew, almond)

▶ Oatcakes with a dollop of nut butter.

EXERCISE: PLANNING BREAKFAST – BE NINJA PREPARED!

Time:
15 minutes

What you'll need:
Pen and paper

Ninja mindset:
Preparedness

Step 1: Fill in this table to plan your Work Fuel breakfasts for the next week. Remember to vary it up a bit so that you're not eating the same breakfast every day!

	How much time will I have (and where will I be?)	Breakfast choice
Monday		
Tuesday		
Wednesday		
Thursday		
Friday		

Step 2: Sometimes the things that get in our way are our existing bad habits. This next step is about eliminating or limiting the fallback options. If you have sugary breakfast cereals or bars in the house, throw them away now!

Step 3: Do you have all the ingredients in the house to make these things? Write a list of any that you need to buy, and go and buy them. (Do you need more eggs? Do you need a container to prepare your overnight oats? If so, get them now!)

Are you a Ninja?

▶ A Ninja knows that breakfast sets the tone for the day's choices and their body's metabolism.

▶ A Ninja is conscious of the Work Fuel essentials at breakfast, like being label-savvy, using caffeine wisely, avoiding the foods with their own jingle, eating the rainbow and creating nutriful, not (always) beautiful meals.

▶ A Ninja steers clear of commercial breakfast cereals that are high in sugar, focusing instead on oats, beans, eggs, smoothies and other options that fill up their Work Fuel Plate.

4.
LUNCH

DITCH THE 'AL DESKO'

When was the last time you took a proper break for lunch? One where you got up from your desk and sat somewhere else. Where you weren't using your left hand to shove forkfuls of food into your mouth while your right hand was tapping away on the keyboard, just finishing off that presentation?

We get it, you have a lot on and those extra 30 minutes are so valuable when you are pressed for time. But that's the thing: you are talking time here; we are talking attention, our most precious and finite resource. The stuff that gets things done. This starts to diminish the further we are from our last break and sometimes that may have been while asleep the previous night.[1]

YOU ARE THE 'WAY' YOU EAT

Your body requires energy and hydration to function properly. That's a fact; it doesn't stop being true just because you're having a busy day at work. And although you may still eat and drink while working, actually taking your lunch break and putting your work on hold for a time increases your productivity, more effectively replenishes your resources, and lowers stress. Let's start to address the 'al desko'. As a key ingredient of the Work Fuel Way, eating at your desk has to go! Why? A bit of background is needed to fully explain.

BACK TO SCIENCE CLASS

Our autonomic nervous system regulates our automatic processes, the things we do without conscious thought – such as our digestion.

For example, we never have to consciously think about breaking down that piece of broccoli bit by bit into digestible molecules; it just hits our stomachs and the process happens automatically, like magic.

One branch of this system is the sympathetic nervous system (SNS). The more common term you are likely to have heard of is 'fight or flight'. The SNS causes our body to release the stress hormones adrenaline and cortisol. The first-released hormone, adrenaline is literally like putting your foot down on the accelerator in the car. It makes the heart beat faster, pushing blood to the muscles and to the heart and other vital organs. Pulse rate and blood pressure go up. Breath rate is increased, so you breathe more rapidly. Small airways in the lungs open wide, to allow the lungs to take in as much oxygen as possible with each breath. Extra oxygen is sent to the brain, increasing alertness. Sight, hearing and other senses become sharper.

Meanwhile, adrenaline is also triggering the release of glucose and fats from temporary storage sites in the body. These nutrients flood into the bloodstream, supplying energy to all parts of the body. All these changes happen instantaneously; the wiring is so efficient that the command centres of the brain – the amygdala and hypothalamus – begin this process before the brain's visual centres have had a chance to fully process what is happening. This is our in-built survival technique and all these bodily responses would make sense if a lion was chasing you. Your muscles and lungs would be more oxygenated to run or fight, and you would suddenly be stronger and faster and have enhanced vision. If the threat is sustained – basically if we didn't get away from said lion – then the next stress hormone, cortisol, is upregulated. This is basically keeping your foot on the accelerator.

WHERE'S THE LION?

But, what does a lion have to do with lunch at your desk? Quite a lot. The lion these days isn't a physical stressor, instead it's more of a psychological one. The lion to us is the email with yet another request from the commercial team; the complex, demanding client call; the VC with your boss in Singapore, and maybe the call that your child is sick at school, and needs picking up, and you are next up on the agenda. Or maybe it's just missing the train and the next one isn't for an hour. Basically, this response can be triggered anytime. While the immediate survival reactions, mentioned above, are kicking in, the body turns off all unnecessary processes, including digestion. It's basically saying, we will digest that salade niçoise later, if there is in fact a later!

Our digestive power, and the enzymes we secrete from our pancreas, are locked away during this time, so we literally can't digest. That perfect salad just sits there waiting in our gut until we are out the other side of the stress response, when all the demands stop. It makes sense as digestion is labour-intensive and trying to stay alive is where the resources are at, like getting blood flow to our muscles. Oh, and that chewed-up food, coated in saliva, has to sit and wait in your gut until you're ready to digest again. This results in brain fog, afternoon slumps and feelings of indigestion (that's what this is by the way – not digesting) – think bloating and cramps.

In Robert Sapolsky's book *Why Zebras Don't Get Ulcers*, he explains that this moment of terror on the savannah is followed by hours of zebra downtime chewing the grass and hanging out with other zebras. What we need more of is that savannah, each day at lunchtime, just like the zebra. It needs to be a calm, sacred, relaxed space to digest in a more efficient and effective fashion, away from any impending lions. By doing this simple act of taking lunch we turn on our parasympathetic nervous system (PSNS), the chilled-out brother of the SNS, known as 'rest and digest'.

REST AND DIGEST

How do we do it? We move away from our screen, from the devices, the people that may sometimes be our lions and we eat lunch in the open air if possible or anywhere that isn't your desk. Even if you think your desk or meeting room isn't stressful, remember, this is an automatic response, not conscious. You cannot mitigate the effect of the next email you may read, the next IM or colleague judgement call you have to make. So, this isn't best practice and that's what we are interested in here: models of excellence, not just getting by. The odds that you will remain in rest and digest mode and not switch to fight or flight while sitting at your desk are not in your favour. Ditch the desk forever.

CREATE CALM

An investment in lunch helps to manage stress, as it creates a calm interruption to the stress cycle in the middle of the day. Repeated stress hormone surges over time can damage blood vessels, increasing blood pressure and raising the risk of heart attacks or strokes. Stress is expensive for our bodies. Elevated cortisol levels create a physiological change that releases energy that is required during the stress response – this is the 'high' of stress – but it also inadvertently causes the buildup of fat tissue and weight gain too. Cortisol increases appetite, so that you will want to eat more to replenish – think emotional over-eating – and it increases the storage of unused nutrients as fat, especially fat around the middle. Taking lunch is a sure-fire way to power up for the afternoon, reset the stress effect, digest properly and feel good in our bodies.

STILL NO TIME FOR LUNCH?

Well, what if we told you that your judgement may be compromised if you don't? An interesting paper in the *Proceedings of the National Academy of Sciences* describes how a team of researchers at Ben-Gurion University of the Negev followed eight Israeli judges for ten months as they ruled on over 1,000 applications made by prisoners to parole boards.[2]

The prisoners were asking either to be allowed out on parole or to have the conditions of their incarceration changed. At the start of the day, the judges granted around two-thirds of the applications before them. As the hours passed, that number fell sharply (see chart), eventually reaching zero. However, more rational decisions returned after the judges stopped for food. After these breaks the approval rate shot back up, before falling again as the hours wore on.

Judgement day
Favourable rulings by parole boards, %

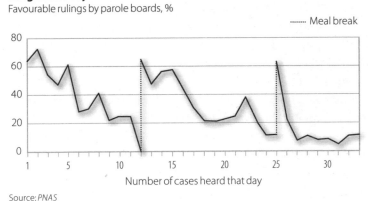

Source: *PNAS*

The researchers hypothesized that blood sugar levels are a crucial variable and that the amount of time since the judge last ate matters in a ruling. Another hypothesis, that was consistent with the results and other studies, is that it was due to the number of cases seen since the last break. Decision-making is mentally taxing. If we are forced to keep deciding things, we get tired and start looking for easy answers. Decision fatigue! In this case, the easy answer was to maintain the status quo by denying the prisoner's request.[3]

Whether it was the blood sugars affecting the decisions or decision fatigue, a lunch break remedies both. What could you be compromising in your working day by not taking a break at lunch? Maybe you are not sending someone to jail, but still, don't chain yourself to your desk. Your judgement, integrity and creative ability are at stake.

COMMON LUNCH TRAPS

Hopefully we have given you something to think about with regard to the importance of taking your lunch break, but what if you are

taking it and falling into some common lunchtime traps? Then we have some ideas, using Ninja tactics to steer you successfully through, protecting your afternoon's productivity. Be a fuelie.

MEAL DEALS

A sandwich, packet of crisps, fizzy drink/ juice and a chocolate bar. We've all done it. They sound appetizing and seem to offer

value for money. But if you're honest, they often contain items you don't actually want to eat and probably wouldn't have chosen if you were paying for each item individually. Plus, a quick look at the labels will reveal that a meal deal lunch is likely to mean you consume more sugars and processed fats than you intended – a big compromise for your attention that afternoon. Use your Ninja ruthlessness and just buy what you actually want to eat. It's no longer value for money when you are feeling sluggish at 3pm and need to get stuff done.

THE *SALAD TRAP*

The word 'salad' is almost always perceived as a healthy option. However, they can be smothered with sugary, processed dressings, topped with fried croutons and laden with pasta or some other simple carb to bulk them out. We have to look beyond the healthy name – the crucial Work Fuel ingredients are likely to be missing. Try being a little unorthodox – swerve the pre-boxed options; instead, select the individual ingredients you want and add in what you know is real fuel.

It's not just salads to be aware of. Food vendors are sneaky. Think about the word 'smoothie' or 'vitamin water' – these sound like good choices, right? Usually not, they are often loaded with hidden sugars and additives.

LEFT IT *TOO LATE*

Your day has run away with you and before you know it, it's 3.30pm and you've yet to have lunch. You're now starving, maybe even a little lightheaded, or feeling anxious and shaky? These are all signs of low blood sugar and your body is sending messages to the brain to eat. The priority now is to ensure you can meet this need. The resulting cravings mean that it's much harder to make a good choice – your willpower will be lowered and if you're not careful you'll end up with a coffee and muffin! Be prepared with back-up snacks that avoid this (see opposite), keeping you away from the vending machine and coffee shop.

HOW TO MAKE A WORK FUEL LUNCH HAPPEN

BRING IT IN

Bringing your own lunch into work puts you into the driving seat. For starters, you choose the ingredients that you like and that you know work for you. Once you have a system in place for doing this, it becomes such an energy-, attention- and time-saving tactic. No more queuing and then having to decide from a limited menu, no more choosing when already half-starved, leaving you open to temptation – just think of all the mental energy wasted on these internal battles that you literally win back when you prep ahead. Besides your home-prepared lunch being extra nutritious, so boosting your energy for the afternoon, the other benefit of a packed lunch is that you don't need a whole hour to track it down, which means you have time to sit and eat – and perhaps a bit of time for a nice walk or a power nap. Just include in your weekly shop a 'take to work' list, including dry or fresh food you can refrigerate or that will last a few days in your desk/bag/car. For example, a bag of leafy greens (rocket, watercress, spinach), cherry tomatoes, hummus, feta cheese, olives, a couple of avocados, tinned or packaged SMASH fish, cold cuts of lean meat and tins of beans.

AUTOMATE YOUR LUNCHES

Prepare your lunches in advance on Sunday, so all you have to do on the day is assemble and go. This way you know what you're eating. See Chapter 8 for more on meal planning, as well as the ideas in the rest of this chapter.

PREP IT IN THE OFFICE

If you have access to a fridge and an office drawer or locker you can do so much. For how to shop for a week of office lunches, check out Chapter 8, and for the toolkit, Chapter 9.

Need to be more inspired? Designer David Bez made a salad at his desk every day for a thousand days and get this, each one was different. His book *Salad Pride* is a testament to this amazing feat and just goes to show that a salad is way more versatile than a lettuce leaf with a soggy tomato and a slice of cucumber.

MAKE IT EASY, THEN EASIER

If you have sweets and biscuits on your desk, you're going to eat them. If you have an apple on your desk, you'll probably eat that instead. If you want to get some healthy fats to fuel your brain, keep some walnuts handy. Bring in your lunch and your bottled water, and put your healthiest snacks closest to hand.[4]

IF YOU'RE GOING OUT, PLAN AHEAD

If you know you're going to lunch with your colleagues or a client and you know where, taking a quick peek at the menu in advance can help you make better choices. That way, you can find an alternative to that spaghetti carbonara or risotto that you know will look and sound so tasty when you haven't eaten in four hours and your body is looking for a quick hit of carbs.

If you are one of the lucky ones that have a good restaurant/café on site that prepares real food options daily, then there's heaps of time saved that you can invest in breakfast and dinner instead. Perhaps you can place your order in advance or plan what you will eat from what's on offer, instead of waiting until you are already hungry.

NEXTOVERS

When cooking or chopping, multiply it every time, so leftovers are by design not by accident, thereby creating nextovers. These are perfect for lunch – you know you are eating something nutritious and you don't have to spend any money (or time) on buying something else.

A typical scenario for making nextovers: the oven is on already, so add in a couple of sweet potatoes, an aubergine and some peppers. They do not need peeling or chopping. Just pop them in on a tray, with some olive oil, salt and pepper. Voila, you have a base for soups, salads, or dinner tomorrow. Have a mantra: 'what can I eat next?' By asking this question each time you are preparing food, it may mean you will not have to cook the next day.

ABOUT COOKING

> 'To cook for the pleasure of it, to devote a portion
> of our leisure to it, is to declare independence from
> the corporations seeking to organize our every
> waking moment into yet another consumption.'
> – Michael Pollan, Cooked

Cooking en masse offers maximum returns. You eat more home-cooked, wholesome food, you save time and it's cost effective too.

We suggest Sunday afternoons are prime time for this – you're (hopefully) not too tired, the week hasn't started and other things are yet to get in the way. Find a time that works for you. Check out these for take-to-work ideas:

▶ **Hard-boiled eggs.** Cook six at a time. Stored in the fridge unpeeled they are good for a week, are very portable, and will super-charge your breakfast and lunch.

▶ **Brown rice/quinoa/barley/lentils.** Cook the whole pack. Throw it all in, then portion it and fridge it or freeze it. This can be eaten hot or cold. Rice is the one to watch here – eat it immediately, or the next day, or freeze it. The others will be OK in the fridge for the entire working week.

▶ **Casseroles, stews, soups, curries, chilli.** Cook for the whole street and again portion it, then fridge it or freeze it. For recipe ideas see pages 221–31.

▶ **Batch chopping.** If chopping a carrot for a recipe, why not chop the whole bag? The chopping board and knife are already out. You can then store them in an airtight container in the fridge. You could eat them as crudités: throw them in your lunch box for work, to eat with hummus or guacamole, or eat as a snack instead of a packet of crisps. This can apply to chopping anything – onions, cucumber, celery. No good at chopping? Get a good knife and check out a YouTube tutorial for chopping skills; there are loads of them. Dice, dice, baby!

Still too much faff?

If the above sound like too much faff at the start, or ever, then you can opt for pre-chopped and pre-cooked. The gold standard, for sure, is chopping and cooking your own; however, some healthy pre-packed food can be very convenient. If it's the difference between you starting to eat more positively or not then some of these are a godsend:

▶ **Frozen goods.** Nowadays you can get so many healthy ingredients from the freezer section, and this means you can always have something in. Items such as chopped onions, minced garlic and ginger, broccoli, cauliflower, peppers, herbs and avocado are great. No chopping and always on hand. Another staple of the freezer is berries and a few smoothie mixes. Beware of the pre-mixed bags, though, as most are high-sugar fruits, so you will need to add extras into the smoothie, as per the Work Fuel formula (page 78).

▶ **Fridge goods.** Like the freezer section, there's lots of healthy convenience here too. Pre-bagged salads/stir-fries/crudités/courgetti. Cooked fish and meats that are vacuum packed are also great to have in: just open and add to the veggies. Prep time is then zero.

▶ **Tinned, jarred and vacuum-packed goods.** Some of the inner aisles of supermarkets contain some quality pre-prepared goodies too. There is a whole selection of pre-cooked brown rice, quinoa, lentils and barley. Do check the labels of these – the first item should be what it says on the front, e.g. quinoa, with perhaps salt, spices and some herbs that are all recognizable foods. If in doubt, check Chapter 6. Tins and jars also offer great long shelf-life options, like beans (not baked) just in water, fish in olive oil, veggies like tomatoes and peppers, and savoury snack items like olives.

With a good stash of the above in the kitchen you can always make something tasty and nourishing for lunch or dinner. Bring it in or prep it at work and start to automate your lunches.

EXERCISE: WHAT SHOULD I EAT FOR LUNCH?

Time:
5–10 minutes

What you'll need:
Pen and paper (or write in the book)
plus good memory recall!

Ninja mindset:
Human not superhero

Colette's typical lunch right back at the start was a cheese baguette with a packet of crisps. This kind of lunch is roughly 75% carbs (the simple, dumb variety at that), with a scrap of protein and fat. Where's the rainbow plants for sustained energy and vitality? The omega-3s for brain power? No surprises she was nodding off during PowerPoint presentations.

Let's do a quick reality check – how does your lunch today stack up to the Work Fuel Plate? Be honest.

Fill in the estimated percentages:
protein, carbs and rainbow plants:

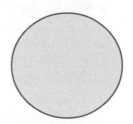

Compare and contrast
with the Work Fuel Plate.

What would you grade yourself – marks out of ten?

Where could you make an instant upgrade?

HERE'S SOME IDEAS:

UPGRADE THE CLASSICS:

Classic	Upgrade
Baked potato and beans	Add cottage cheese and a rainbow salad
Sandwich and crisps	Make it a convertible (1 slice of bread), add extra protein (e.g. boiled egg, tinned fish) and greens, bag of popcorn
Sushi box	Opt for sashimi instead of rolls (less white rice) and add a rainbow salad

WORK FUEL PLATE LUNCH FORMULA

Rather than us prescribing your lunch, engineer your own by following the five steps opposite. The possibilities are endless – well, almost. The quantities are designed for one person.

> ● **REMEMBER THIS** ●
>
> Make a dressing in one minute:
>
> 3 tbsp extra virgin olive oil
>
> 1 tbsp vinegar (balsamic, apple cider or other wine vinegar)
>
> Pinch of salt and pepper
>
> You can add in a teaspoon of mustard, honey or any spice you like (suggestions of brain-enhancing varieties opposite). Double or triple the ingredients to make more for the fridge.

Step 1	Step 2	Step 3	Step 4	Step 5
Choose your leafy greens – 2 large mix 'n' match handfuls (100 g)	Choose a protein – palm-sized amount (75 g)	Choose your rainbow veggies – 2 large mix 'n' match handfuls (100 g)	Choose your smarter carbs – palm-sized amount (75 g)	Choose a topping – 2 tbsp
• Watercress	• Cooked chicken	• Tomatoes	• Quinoa	• Sauerkraut
• Rocket	• Tinned/cooked fish	• Avocado	• Brown rice	• Spicy kimchi
• Spinach	• Cooked tofu	• Beetroot	• Any nextovers – roasted root veggie?	• Kefir dressing (see recipe, page 233)
• Kale	• Cooked beef	• Peppers	• Lentils	• Toasted seeds
• Steamed broccoli	• Cooked turkey	• Cucumber	• Black beans	• Toasted nuts
• Shredded cabbage	• Feta cheese (50 g)	• Onion	• Cold new potatoes	• Guacamole
• Romaine lettuce	• Boiled eggs × 2	• Carrots	• Falafel (see recipe, page 221)	• Spiced hummus (see recipe, page 232)

LUNCH IDEAS

If you would like some tasty road-tested ideas, just add the following options to a base of dark leafy greens and rainbow salad. You could even make it a convertible sandwich (top off, one slice of bread) with some real bread. You could batch chop all the veggies at the start of the week; they will last three to five days refrigerated and in a sealed container, except tomatoes – throw cherry tomatoes in whole. Oh, and keep your cucumber chunky (it goes watery and soggy very quickly). Feel free to add any nutritious nextovers to these ideas too:

Gone for Lunch!

> **Omega-3 niçoise** – add together green beans (lightly cooked or tinned), 4–6 new potatoes (cold), 1–2 boiled eggs and a tinned or vacuum-packed portion of salmon/mackerel.

> **Feta** – add an 80 g portion of crumbled feta to red onion, roasted and chopped sweet potato and beetroot, and stir in cold cooked quinoa. Or add a few tablespoons of chickpeas.

> **Hot smoked salmon and avocado** – with two or three oatcakes.

> **Falafel and hummus** (recipe provided for both of these on pages 221 and 232 or buy prepared – just check the ingredients).

> **Halloumi and walnut** – add either a cup of quinoa or oatcakes.

> **Mixed bean, beetroot and tuna salad** – take a tin of mixed beans, a tin of tuna, add in a chopped cooked beetroot (vacuum packed in natural juice), spice it up with any herbs (coriander/

mint/parsley) you fancy, lemon, olive oil and vinegar and mix together.

Soup – buy or make a fresh vegetable-based soup. Not canned! Look for protein levels of 15 g per serving. Add to this two or three oatcakes with hummus/guacamole/chopped boiled egg.

Egg travel muffin – see recipe on page 217.

Yes, we did just say make your own soup there. It's easier than you think to make a huge vat of it and saves so much money. It's basically a cooked salad (veggies, protein and herb) with stock. There are a few ideas on pages 222–4 to start you off.

SPICES DON'T JUST MAKE FOOD TASTE BETTER, THEY MAKE FOOD BETTER FOR YOU

We encourage you to stock up and create an extensive spice cupboard. Spices are basically a cheap superfood. There are a few spices that are worth noting because they promote brain power. Add liberally and experiment in your soups; on top of salads; when cooking fish, meat and veggies; in smoothies (cayenne, ginger and turmeric all work well) or perhaps even as a natural flavour for your water bottle.

Ginger

Ginger may help enhance memory and improve key indicators of cognitive function, suggests a Thai study.[5] Throw a 3 cm chunk of fresh ginger into your smoothie or chop into curries for a cognition punch.

Sage

The clue is in the name; 'sage' literally means wise, learned and intelligent. Sage the herb contains compounds that may help to sharpen the mind and improve memory and recall. Some people also find that it helps to clear and calm the mind, making focusing easier.[6] Add a few sage leaves to your favourite soups, sauces and stews.

Rosemary

Rosemary is known to increase blood flow to your brain and strengthen memory and concentration. Carnosic acid, present in rosemary leaf, has been shown to fight free-radical damage in the brain too.[7] Plus, it makes most roasted dishes taste and look like a chef has been involved.

Cinnamon

Research shows that just smelling cinnamon can enhance cognitive processing and it has been shown to improve scores on tasks related to attention, memory and visual-motor speed.[8]

Cayenne

This whips up heat and taste in dishes, but effectively boosts the nutrition too. Cayenne has been found to be helpful to the digestion of other nutrients. It's a circulatory stimulant and helps you feel fuller quicker. You can add cayenne to almost any dish, even smoothies. Start with a sprinkle to check your tolerance and then add a little more to taste.[9]

Turmeric

Not a day goes by, it seems, when turmeric is not revealed to have another amazing property. In recent years, more than 5,000 articles have been published in medical literature about curcumin alone, the pigment that gives it its yellow colour. It has a pungent, bitter taste that not everyone likes; however, it's easy to disguise. Research has shown that there is a possibility that it could help improve memory and make you smarter. Add black pepper, as it boosts absorption.[10]

Are you a Ninja?

▶ A Ninja ignores those that say 'lunch is for wimps', ditches the 'al desko' and takes lunch seriously.

▶ A Ninja adopts a 'preparedness mindset' to make eating a good lunch at work easy – prepping at the start of the week, focusing on food that is portable, and batch cooking or over-cooking for dinner to bring in nextovers.

▶ A Ninja takes a break to eat, knowing that the 'how' is almost as important as the 'what' when it comes to digestion and energy.

5.
DINNER

WIN THE DAY, NOW WIN THE EVENING TOO

You get home later than you planned, or you are working from home and those last emails took a little longer than you anticipated. You are now starving, you walk

'After a good dinner, one can forgive anybody, even one's own relations.'
– Oscar Wilde

into the kitchen, open the fridge and … 'argh, there's nothing to eat!'

Ever happened to you? It's happened to us, resulting in a good fifteen minutes of aimless searching and then eventually settling for a cereal dinner, tuna eaten out of the can or, worse, a takeaway! OK, so this type of behaviour isn't going to kill us, at least not if this is an exception – plus there are certainly healthier options for takeaways these days. However, let's start viewing making the right choices at dinner time as the icing on the cake of a successful, productive day.

Eating late (one to two hours before bed)[1] or at irregular times, and eating too much can affect our ability to sleep well. It's also linked to memory function, and attention levels the next day and could cause you to feel hungrier than usual in the morning, affecting your eating the next day.[2] If we end on a high the foundations are set for a good night's sleep and even better results for tomorrow. In this chapter we're going to focus on your dinner at home strategy. Eating out or while away will be covered in Chapter 7.

FIRST STEP, CREATING MORE ORDER

In both of our coaching experiences we have often come across disordered eating, which is not to be confused with eating disorders such as anorexia or bulimia. Instead it's the erratic way people find feeding windows within their working week. One day breakfast, the next nothing; one day lunch is at 4pm, then non-existent for the rest of the week; a day of fasting (not on purpose) followed by an all-day buffet and so on. The occasional erratic day is fine, but day after day it's just not sustainable. Establishing eating patterns that are stuck to the majority of the time supports better metabolism, energy levels and sleep patterns, whereas unusual/irregular food intake induces the opposite.[3]

> ● **REMEMBER THIS** ●
>
> When you eat is just as important as what you eat. Dinner should be eaten at least two hours before bed.[4] Ideally it should *not* be our main meal of the day; a stronger breakfast and lunch should result in a smaller plate for dinner. Why? Earlier in the day our bodies are better equipped for digesting and metabolizing food. Eating late has been shown to lower morning and afternoon energy levels and lower our tolerance to sugar.[5]

Increasingly, research is showing that we should narrow the window in which we eat. In doing so we are giving our body a chance to reset and recalibrate, which equals more energy, better immunity, a happier gut, mental clarity and overall bet-  ter health. All of this is achieved by literally giving the body a break from digesting for a significant period of time, allowing it time to invest in other areas like gut maintenance.

LET'S TALK ABOUT TIME-RESTRICTED FEEDING (TRF)

I think we already knew that midnight snacking wasn't a Productivity Ninja's go-to regime, but what time-restricted feeding does is give you a more precise time window in which to eat (or not). This can vary anywhere from twelve-hour eating windows, all the way to four hours and in some cases even less. The window starts when you first ingest something that isn't water or toothpaste and ends when you last do the same. A note of caution here: for some people, skipping meals and severely limiting calories can be dangerous for their pre-existing conditions, for example diabetes, or for those on medications for blood pressure or heart disease. Different fasting approaches warrant a whole other book altogether, but for the purpose of this book we would like to introduce the minimum effective time span of twelve hours.

In the twelve-hour window, an example would be commencing breakfast at 8am and having dinner all finished by 8pm. Simple eh? Can you stick to this every day? The research has indicated that this window is still protective against metabolic diseases, even when briefly interrupted on weekends. And as a bonus, it helps with sleep too. We really do not need a huge meal before bed, resulting in lots of sleep-disrupting insulin circulating, so bringing dinner forward to meet the window supports the quality of our rest too.

'I fast for greater physical and mental efficiency.'
– Plato

The food that we would normally eat after dinner and before bed is typically sugary; it's when our willpower is at its lowest. So, make this a rule: stop eating at dinner and don't eat until breakfast. It's easy to stick to if you have the same order every day.[6]

Hara hachi bu!
Hara hachi bu is the Okinawan 2,500-year-old Confucian mantra said before meals to remind them to stop eating when their stomachs are 80% full. The 20% gap between not being hungry and feeling full could be the difference between losing weight or gaining it, feeling vibrant or tired, optimally digesting your food or not. People living in 'Blue Zones', the areas of the world in which people live the longest, eat their smallest meal in the late afternoon or early evening

and then they don't eat any more for the rest of the day. If it's been tried and tested for 2,500 years by the longest-living communities, then this TRF stuff is definitely worth a go.

Curb the snacks

So we now have a feeding window. What, then, about snacks during this time? Unlimited? The answer is, *not unless you want the gremlins*. OK, the correct term is ghrelin, but gremlin makes more sense to us. It's the hormone that tells us to eat, like a little gremlin in our bodies asking for food. The more feeding times we have, the more elevated this hormone is – you give it more, it asks for more. When we are grazing all day, we are digesting all day too. As we have already described, this is labour-intensive. By giving our gut a break it allows the digestive system to do a bit of maintenance work and our gut bacteria some time to flourish. This is very good for energy levels too. Guilia Enders, in her book *Gut*, describes how the stomach rumbling is a very good sign – it is basically our gut letting us know that it has been given sufficient time to recover from the last food parcel. It's a sign of happiness and function. Here's a question – when was the last time your stomach (it's actually the small intestine, but that's a minor detail) rumbled?

With three balanced meals per day, the need for snacking is diminished. Most snacks are 'just because' snacks anyhow: just because you're bored; you're watching a film; it's left over; it's someone's birthday (again) in the office, etc. When adjusting, you don't have to go cold turkey, just gradually bolster your main meals and wean yourself off the snacks. You are human not superhero, so it's not an overnight change.

Exceptions: Snack if …
▶ You are still at work at 7.30pm and haven't eaten since lunch.

▶ You are doing some serious exercise that day that is likely to consume a lot of energy.

▶ You are crossing time zones and meals are all over the place.

▶ You are truly hungry, not dehydrated, you already checked that.

Snack on
▶ An apple with nut butter

▶ Half an avocado with some lemon and salt

▶ A handful of walnuts with some berries

▶ Crudités/vegetable sticks with dips or nut butters

▶ Oatcakes with dips or nut butters

▶ Fruit and nut bars (be label-savvy)

▶ Mackerel on rye/spelt/sourdough toast

▶ Homemade energy bites – see the Work Fuel formula on page 117 or check out the recipe for Chocolate Power Bites on page 231

▶ Boiled egg

▶ Organic live plain/Greek/plant yoghurt.

Chew, chew and chew again!
Our bodies are extremely interconnected, and many processes start in the mouth. The simple act of chewing has many mechanisms attached to it: not just digestion but hormone pathways, jaw muscle, teeth health and our gut microbiome. The more we chew, the more efficient and effective our digestion is, which equals less energy spent on breaking down unchewed food and more energy for us.[7]

We have teeth for a reason! It's also the reason that we recommend if you are making a smoothie you save some of the ingredients to chew before you drink it, or why if you have smooth soup you should think of serving a salad or something crunchy on the side. If we swallow our food with little or no chews, which is often the case if we are distracted – by the TV or scanning social media – then we may miss out on this crucial step. This contributes to inefficient digestion, discomfort and fatigue.

EXERCISE: COUNT THE CHEW

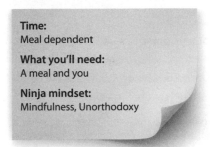

Time:
Meal dependent

What you'll need:
A meal and you

Ninja mindset:
Mindfulness, Unorthodoxy

Step 1: The next time you sit down for dinner, count how many times you are chewing food before swallowing it. Count at least four or five mouthfuls, so you have a good baseline measure. Granted, this depends on what type of food you are eating and how much you put in your mouth at once, but still, it's interesting to know the baseline.

Step 2: Now switch to chewing each mouthful 30 times; do it at least ten times.

Step 3: What did you notice after chewing for longer? How did you feel during and after the meal? Did you eat less or more?

A Chinese study found that our food intake was 11.9% lower after 40 chews than after fifteen chews.[8] The Japanese government's Ministry of Health are so convinced of the health benefits of chewing, that they proposed a public health campaign to encourage people to chew each mouthful of their food 30 times.[9] In the early 1900s, a self-proclaimed 'economic nutritionist' named Horace Fletcher recommended chewing each bite to the point of liquefaction – around 100 times. This creates involuntary swallowing. While we are not suggesting the 100 mark, can you set yourself a personal target of chews to aim for?

If more chewing equals more energy, that seems like an obvious free and immediate upgrade to us.

When you eat, just eat.
Don't be walking around the house doing the laundry or be distracted by the TV. Give it your full attention. The very process of digestion begins with smell, sights, sounds and thoughts of food. Why hinder it by being distracted by something else?

• REMEMBER THIS •

How would you eat dinner if you had (a) guest(s)? We are guessing at a table, offline, with a knife and a fork, taking time to enjoy it and pausing between mouthfuls. This is how we should eat dinner every night.

WHAT TO EAT FOR DINNER

The good news is that a lot of the classic dinner options are already pretty good. With just a few tweaks here and there, they start to echo the Work Fuel Way with minimal effort and are likely to taste better too. Check these out:

UPGRADE THE CLASSICS

Classic	Upgrade
Shepherd's pie	Swap the mash for sweet potato mash or a mix of cauliflower and potato. Add extra carrots and onions to the sauce.
Macaroni cheese	Choose wholemeal macaroni and add in tomatoes, peas and broccoli.
Spaghetti bolognaise	Swap white pasta for black bean or wholewheat pasta or courgetti (courgette noodles), add in mushrooms, onions and carrots to the sauce.

Classic	Upgrade
Mashed potato	Try mock mash: a tin of cannellini beans and cauliflower – once cooked, blend, season and add butter to taste.

WORK FUEL DINNERS

Rainbow curry with quinoa – These days shop-bought curry pastes and pre-packed mixes are of a pretty high standard. If you like curry, then stock up on a few different blends. They last ages in the cupboard and bring other dishes alive too, like beans, eggs and fish. We have a simple recipe for you try on page 228. You can cook the quinoa yourself, or buy a pre-cooked option – just be label-savvy.

Chilli with brown rice – Disguised in a delicious, well-seasoned tomato base, you can sneak in lots of veggies (great when the kids or the other half doesn't want to eat them and you need a little Ninja stealth and camouflage! Our record is ten). Chilli doesn't have to be a meaty affair: you make a giant pan of a veggie version, then you can add meat/fish or even eggs at different meals, changing it up. Plus, you get to use most of the top brain spices in this one and you could cook once and eat all week in different guises. Brown rice can be cooked from dry or use a pre-cooked packet – just check the label for nasties.

Eight-veg ratatouille – This is a very versatile dish. Eaten on its own it's a little low in protein, so serve with grilled fish, chicken, turkey or steak, or add beans/lentils. Recipe on page 226.

Fishcakes or black bean burger – A perfect batch-cook item, you can make ten or more at a time and freeze. See recipe, page 229. You can of course buy these ready-made, just remember, be label-savvy.

FINALLY, I HAVE JUST WALKED IN AND I AM STARVING. NO CHANCE OF COOKING ...

Brain bowl – 5 minutes

This one involves no cooking, the ingredients are the recipe:

½ an avocado

50–100 g smoked salmon

2 tbsp cottage cheese

Handful of dark leafy greens

½ cucumber

1 chopped beetroot (vacuum packed).

Don't eat fish? Substitute feta or seeds/chopped nuts or tinned beans of your choice and maybe add a wedge of sourdough toast too.

There is only one suggested cold dish in our evening meals: this is intentional. Raw food requires a higher digestive capacity. This tends to wane as the day goes on (as we do). Since cooked food is easier to digest, it helps us to wind down and set us up for that all-important restful night.

WHAT ABOUT SOMETHING SWEET?

You may have realized we haven't mentioned desserts. As you are loading your plate with real fuel you will notice you are less likely to fancy something sweet after a meal. At least, the more you do it, that is!

But if you do really fancy something, opt for:

▶ A few squares of dark chocolate, choose 70%+ cocoa.

▶ A couple of dates stuffed with nut butter

▶ One-ingredient banana ice cream – yep, just frozen bananas, blended – serve immediately!

▶ A handful of berries with yoghurt

▶ Fruit crumble – basically any stewed fruit of your choice, topped with nuts, cinnamon and yoghurt

▶ Or try making your own delicious energy bites – see below for the instructions and formula.

Energy Bite Formula

1	2	3	4
Choose your nuts (150 g)	**Choose your dried fruit (200 g)**	**Choose your binder (1–2 tbsp)**	**Choose your coating**
• Walnuts	• Dates	• Nut butter	• Chia seeds
• Almonds	• Raisins	• Tahini	• Cacao
• Cashew	• Apricots	• Coconut oil	• Shredded coconut
• Sunflower seeds	• Figs	• Water	• Crushed nuts

There are hundreds of ways to create different energy bites; they are guaranteed to satisfy any sweet cravings, and with their fibre, fat and protein content they actually feed you too – unlike most pre-wrapped so-called health bars. Simply choose an ingredient from each category (a combination from the same category is fine too, just keep to proportions). Then whizz together in a blender or food processor and shape into balls. These measurements should make around twenty. Roll the balls in the coating and firm them up in the fridge for an hour or the freezer for fifteen minutes. If your mixture is a little too dry you can add a little water, or more of your binder option, one tablespoon at a time. These can be kept in the fridge for a week or so; you can even freeze them.

There are also days when only cake will do, so on those days eat the cake. Consistency beats intensity, especially when it comes to cake. If most of the time you are not eating it, then having a slice (or two) when you really want to isn't going to derail you.

Are you a Ninja?

▶ A Ninja is always thinking a step ahead, so finishes the day with a warm, satisfying meal that sets up a good night's sleep.

▶ A Ninja knows that these kinds of meal don't have to be extravagant or complicated, and isn't afraid to cut corners.

▶ A Ninja avoids the late-night snacks so as to give the best chance of the body having at least twelve hours of fasting time before tomorrow's breakfast.

6.
BEING LABEL-SAVVY

IT'S TIME TO **RECONNECT WITH OUR FOOD**

Living in modern times, it's likely you'll find yourself in situations where your only food option is something from a packet. We want you to be Ninja prepared in this situation, and label-savvy. That's why we're giving you this chapter.

Industrialized food is a relatively recent development; only in the last hundred years have we really started to see bulk-manufacturing of foods. Real food, the food from plants and animals, represents thousands of years of adaptation and evolution for life on our glorious planet. Regardless of what our minds might tell us when we see that cleverly packaged ready meal, what our brains would choose every time is nutrient-rich, natural, biologically active foods.

IF FOOD NEEDS A MARKETING TEAM TO CONVINCE US IT'S WORTH EATING, IT'S PROBABLY NOT WORTH EATING

Modern food manufacturers have clever marketing techniques to make their foods and products sound like healthy and good-value choices, but more often than not, this is not the case.

The labels on products have become increasingly complex and, in some cases, misleading. With the ever-changing diet culture, what should we be focusing on anyway when we look at labels? The calories, the macros, the RDAs, the traffic light? Per serving or per 100 g?

This is even assuming they have been labelled correctly in the first place – recent headlines have shown that there are some manufacturers that are underreporting levels of things like sugar and hydrogenated fats in their foods.[1] They already have a 20% leeway as it is, so even the most committed calorie counter is never quite as accurate as they think they are.

Well, we think life is complicated enough without having to be a food scientist to manage such calculations at every meal, so unless you are a dedicated athlete trying to achieve precise outcomes, then simply focusing on avoiding highly processed foods is the best advice we can give you. How to do this? By eating real, single-ingredient foods most of the time. If some of the time it does have a label, be savvy.

This seems obvious, yet in a study by the University of São Paulo of nineteen European countries, it was found that UK families buy ultra-processed food amounting to 50.7% of the diet – the most in Europe. It's scary that we are eating more and more of these foods, as just a 10% increase in the proportion of ultra-processed foods in the diet is associated with an increase of 12% in the risk of overall cancer, and with an 11% increase in the risk of breast cancer. This ultra-processed concept is relatively new. It refers to foods that have many additives such as preservatives, sweeteners, sensory enhancers, colourants and processing aids, but sadly little or no real food.[2]

While the manufacturers are required to be truthful (within a 20% margin, remember) and only use food additives and ingredients that have been approved for consumption, there is scope to distort. Crafty marketing techniques may highlight certain features of the food items, tricking us into thinking we are making a great, healthy choice. For example, labelling an apple juice as 'fat free': apples are naturally fat free – labelling the product as such is a totally irrelevant health claim. In fact, apple juice contains extremely high amounts of sugar that we just do not need to consume. Words such as 'natural' can also be confusing. A fruit juice concentrate as a sweetener is natural, but nevertheless very high in sugar, and a healthy-looking granola may contain high quantities of 'natural' fruit sugars, meaning you end up with a very different result than the one you planned for. Rather than a nourishing, energizing breakfast, a sugar-laden granola may cause rollercoaster energy spikes and dips for most of the morning, and will likely result in an additional snack needing to be consumed by 10am.

BEING LABEL-SAVVY

Being label-savvy just requires knowing a few basic rules of the road. Read our eight before you add them to your plate:

1. **Fewer than five ingredients.** The more ingredients there are, the further the food is likely to be from the real food source, therefore not a good Work Fuel choice. If there are more than five, then chances are it is going down the highly processed route. There are exceptions to this, naturally, so employ rule two as a backup if it still looks promising.

2. **If you can't pronounce it, don't eat it!** Simple. If manufacturers don't want us to easily identify what's in a product, they probably have something to hide.

3. **Look at the order that foods appear in in the ingredients list.** Foods are listed by weight order, with the food that makes up the largest proportion of the food appearing first. Be wary of any sugars/omega-6 oils (sunflower, corn, soybean) or trans fats if they appear at the beginning of the list, as these will make up the largest proportion of the food.

4. **Use the per 100 g column.** This establishes a level playing field. The per serving column is often used to disguise the amount of sugar, fat or salt that a food contains. The portion sizes used are often unrealistically small; for example, the servings listed on packs of cereal are usually 25 g or 30 g, which looks tiny in our standard bowls – we are more likely to serve double or triple this.

5. **If it has a health claim, avoid.** The claims are dubious at best and terms such as 'natural' and 'healthy' are ill-defined words that have no legal or formal meaning. Manufacturers can get away with using them without being accused of breaching advertising or labelling regulations.

6. **Look for the 'ose'.** These are the disguised added sugars – glucose, fructose, maltose, dextrose or lactose; quite simply, anything ending in 'ose' is a simple sugar and should be avoided in large quantities. Sugar added to foods can also be disguised with other names for sugar, including honey, syrup, nectar sugar or even healthy-sounding fruit juice concentrate. Low sugar foods will contain 5 g or less per 100 g.

7. **Dodge high-fructose corn syrup (HFCS).** This sugar has its own mention, as it is now found in so many processed foods including fizzy drinks, sweets, sweetened yoghurts, salad dressings, sauces, condiments, breakfast cereals and granola bars, and even bread. It is a highly processed sugar derived from corn and it is very quickly released into the bloodstream after consumption, playing havoc with our precious blood sugar balance and energy levels, slaying our concentration, mood and attention levels. Not to mention that it can also lead to an increased risk of diabetes and obesity.[3]

8. **Understand the per 100 g breakdown.** Of course, our aim is to move away from processed food as much as possible. But if you end up in a situation where it's the only option, then these figures give you a guide to what's a high or low content for things like fats and sugars.

Per 100 g	High	Low
Total fat	more than 17.5 g	3 g or less
SATURATED FAT	more than 5 g	1.5 g or less
Sugars	more than 22.5 g of total sugars	5 g of total sugars or less
Salt	more than 1.5 g of salt (or 0.6 g sodium)	0.3 g of salt or less (0.1 g sodium)

EXERCISE: HOW LABEL-SAVVY ARE YOU?

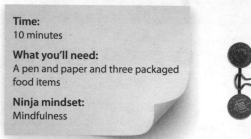

Time:
10 minutes

What you'll need:
A pen and paper and three packaged
food items

Ninja mindset:
Mindfulness

Step 1: Write down three packaged foods that you have recently eaten.

Step 2: For each of the three food items, without checking, write down what you think the answers are to the following:

▶ The first ingredient listed (therefore the biggest by weight ingredient)

▶ The total number of ingredients

▶ Amount of total sugars.

Step 3: Now go and check the pack (or website); how did you do? Be honest.

Are you a Ninja?

▶ A Ninja is sceptical about marketing claims and avoids foods that are so processed that they need their own jingle to make you buy them.

▶ A Ninja is label-savvy and checks the ingredients list for nasties, such as things that end in 'ose', and things that sound like factory-made preservatives or additives.

▶ A Ninja looks for foods that follow the 'five-ingredient rule' – and knows that the best foods have only one item on their ingredients list!

7.
THRIVING ON
THE GO

If there's one thing that is going to sabotage your efforts, it's skipping meals due to your on-the-go schedule. Likewise grabbing food on the run. When we are already hungry and stressed, we seek out the path

'Successful people form habits that feed their success, instead of habits that feed their failure.'
– Jeff Olson

of least resistance, a snack from a vending machine, a shop en route to the next appointment or a coffee-with-baguette grab. While this will fill a gap in the short term, it's far from convenient – you'll find yourself feeling hungry again after a short amount of time and this is anything but Work Fuel. Next stop: brain fog, falling asleep in meetings and maybe stomach ache! Don't compromise.

BE NINJA PREPARED

You eat good food if you see, have and own it! Simple. It's no surprise that sales of fruit and vegetables increase if they are placed at the till point. Have the food to hand, whether that's in the fridge at home, at your desk at work or in your bag if you're on the run.

And on those days when you do not know what the catering situation will be – perhaps at a conference or when you're travelling all day – then load up on breakfast, adding an extra egg, a smoothie or another couple of tablespoons of Greek yoghurt to the usual.

PORTABLES

The portables are foods that are convenient to carry, durable and quick to pack.

VEGETABLES AND FRUIT

Unsurprisingly, vegetables top the list of the best portable, healthy, nutrient-rich foods to satisfy hunger. This kind of food you just can't get out of a vending machine; you are going to have to have these with you.

Prep ahead: Chop them up into crudités, pick up a bagged salad, a box of cherry tomatoes or pack the leftovers from last night's dinner.

Pick up a pack of berries, buy a bag of apples at the start of the week to keep in the car, or chop a few different fruits, add to a jar and pop in your bag.

EGGS

The ultimate fast food. Eggs are the ideal food to satisfy cravings and help you to feel mentally focused, while also providing plenty of other essential nutrients. Boiled eggs are an ideal snack to eat on the go along with some crudité vegetables like peppers, cherry tomatoes or carrot sticks. Boil six eggs at a time: they keep for a week in the fridge unpeeled.

Prep ahead: Make a batch of egg travel muffins for the entire week – see recipe, page 217.

GREEK YOGHURT

Prep ahead: Pop it in a jar and top with nuts and berries and bring from home, or just pack it separately, but ready to assemble. You can even buy on the go, with a bag of nuts and a piece of fruit, and use the yoghurt pot to eat from. A perfect airport snack.

HOMEMADE ENERGY BITES

Making your own portable chocolatey, nutty snack allows you to control the ingredients and avoid too much sugar. Many of the shop-bought so-called 'healthy' energy bars are little more than glorified sweets. They tend to be loaded with sugar, or unpronounceable additives. Be label–savvy and check the sugars (see page 125). Does your favourite go-to snack meet the Work Fuel criteria?

Prep ahead: Make a whole tray of our no-bake energy bites – recipe on page 117. The recipe makes around twenty portions. They keep for at least a week in the fridge, or you could even freeze them. They take around twenty minutes to make; that's one minute per superfood snack. It would take you much longer to find a shop, purchase the chocolate bar and leave. Now who is trading in the false economy?

If you want to save time buying the ingredients, in some supermarkets you can find the pre-mixed ingredients that you then just need to portion out and roll into balls.

SMOOTHIES

Prep ahead: These can be pre-made the day before, refrigerated and put in a heat-protective container to take with you. It's not suitable for air travel hand luggage as it's a liquid; however, a top tip if you have check-in luggage is to freeze the smoothie the night before, and store it in your luggage in the hold. By the time you arrive at your destination it's a chilled, nutritious meal. One less thing to worry about on arrival.

AVOCADO

This is the ultimate travel food comrade. Colette has opened avocados using all sorts of instruments, including her business card. Now she carries a small reusable spoon and knife that are permanently in her work bag (see Chapter 9: 'Toolkit'). It's like a mini meal. Spread it on an oatcake – these often come in handy small packs of five – or mix and match with the other food available where you are. For example, pick a brown bread egg sandwich from the buffet, discard half of the bread, add the avocado on top. You may even make new friends: many a conversation has been started at conference when someone asks Colette what she is doing with her business card.

TINNED FISH

Carry a small tin with you, and you have an instant upgrade of any meal you can find.

> **● REMEMBER THIS ●**
>
> Your cunning plan comes to fruition – you take your own lunch on the road, consisting of real, tasty food you prepared at home. Nextovers! Relish that smug feeling: you were right to be Ninja prepared. The food choices on offer are rubbish and you cleverly pull out of your bag a first-class lunch and everyone's face drops in amazement. Followed by questions about what it is, and how you made it. Bask in your moment of glory!

AIR *TRAVEL*

Plane meals are generally terrible Work Fuel. They're made from fake foods and only taste OK because they're full of bad fats, salt and sugar. It's worth switching your mindset. The first step is to be choosy about what you're given on the flight. The next step is to upgrade your meals, by adding some of the portables we've just mentioned. The final step is to say no to the plane meal altogether and rely only on what you bring with you. We get that this isn't always possible, but it's something to aim for.

Packing even one thing is better than none. Maybe to start it's just your water bottle that you fill once past security, or an apple.

CARRY-ON PLANE FOOD IDEAS:

► Two boiled eggs

► Avocado

► Pack of oatcakes

► Dark chocolate

► Apple

► Pack of berries

► Pack of nuts

► Water bottle.

• REMEMBER THIS •

Order a special meal on flights. A vegetarian or vegan option generally gets you more rainbow plants and something that looks a little less processed. Graham likes to order either 'Asian vegetarian' or 'Hindu vegetarian'. He's not a Hindu, but there's no law that says you need to be (he just gets some funny looks and double-checking when the flight crew brings it over!). This kind of meal tends to include a vegetable-based dish with fruit and salad sides. Add in your own avocado and you end up with a pretty passable meal.

If you didn't get a chance to pack or pick up any good options in the airport, then pick a high-protein meal option, with any salad or fruits available. Stick with water (and drink as much of it as you can), as caffeine and alcohol dehydrate you. If you step off a plane and feel like crap, it's probably because you're dehydrated. It's drier than the Sahara on a flight. Drink around 250 ml of water per hour of flight, and increase this if you are drinking alcohol.

HOTEL BREAKFASTS

Swerve the funky fruit juice dispensers, avoid the cereal jars and sandwich breads and leave the pastries on the tray. Instead, opt for the most protein-rich and colourful options – eat the rainbow. Think back to our examples in Chapter 3:

▶ Eggs plus as many veggies as possible – tomatoes, beans, mushrooms, spinach

▶ Fresh fruit salad, topped with nuts, seeds and natural yoghurt

▶ If they have good bread (real stuff you slice yourself, has some weight to it and is dark in colour), toast it and top it with protein and rainbow colours

▶ If nothing of this general theme is available, hydrate, grab a banana and a handful of the walnuts you pre-packed, *or* skip it until you can get something decent.

● **REMEMBER THIS** ●

Both of us have travelled extensively on business and found that it is very rare to not be able to get some variant of the above at a hotel. If there is nothing suitable, just make a special request for something – ask for a couple of boiled eggs and tomatoes; you may be nicely surprised. If you don't ask, you don't get fed.

BRAVING IT EMPTY HANDED

Being Ninja prepared is essential to the Work Fuel Way – there is always something you can carry with you. A boiled egg, an apple and a pack of walnuts fit into anyone's bag. Even if you are not starting off your trip from home, pocket some extras at the hotel breakfast or even ask for a takeaway lunch bag: lots of hotels will prepare this for you – just be sure to give them some guidance on what you want in it. It's important to have a fuel plan – you never know when there will be a rail strike, a three-hour delay on our flight or a traffic jam.

However, we know that there are scenarios where this just doesn't work out. In these instances, use the Work Fuel Plate as a guide and ask these three questions:

1. Any rainbow fruit and vegetables you can source?

2. Any SMASH (sardines, mackerel, anchovies, salmon, herring) on offer?

3. Anything protein-rich?

The answer is, most of the time there is – even in (we hate to say it) McDonald's. OK, the salad will not be as fresh as we would like, the protein source questionable, but it's a better option than a Big Mac and fries! For every food outlet, question the carbs they will feed you – usually refined and full of trans fats. Unpick the meals they serve and piece together a better one.

EATING OUT? ORDER FIRST, SET THE TREND

For some of us, dinners out are just par for the course. From personal experience we know that the more people we dine out with, the more we eat. However, the journal *Nutrition* studied this behaviour and came up with some precise statistics. When we eat even with just one person we eat 33% more than when we dine alone. This increases to 47% more with three people and a whopping 96% increase when seven or more people are present. That means we eat almost twice as much when we dine with a big group.[1] There are a few reasons proposed as to why this is the case. Firstly, we tend to eat for longer periods when in a big group – more minutes usually means more food. We also tend to order more than we may do ordinarily, to share, meaning there is more available to eat.[2]

Going to bed with a full stomach disrupts our rest time, which doesn't sound very Ninja-like. So, order first. The person that orders first sets the tone for the whole table. If the first person orders burgers and fries, it makes it harder for you to stick to your Work Fuel plan, as we mentally justify eating the deep-fried, no-nutrition fries by the fact that 'they are having it too' or 'my order isn't as bad as hers' type of thing.[3]

This is known as anchoring. Whoever drops the anchor first, just like a boat in the sea, people will circle around that. Drop your anchor on proper food and you set the tone for the whole table. Check out how your wise choices positively influence those around you when next at dinner.

This applies to dessert too. Just think back to all those times when the waiting staff turn up with dessert menus and ask the question: 'Any desserts or coffees?' If your answer is 'No thanks, it's late and I don't need the sugar or caffeine before bed, but can I have a peppermint tea please?', you will (hopefully) set a trend for your colleagues who follow.

RESTAURANT MENU **SURVIVAL TACTICS**

STARTER

Salads or soups are smart, nutritious options and can help bolster your willpower when the fries arrive, as you will already be more satisfied. They are packed with fibre and water, which help fill you up. Ask for the dressing on the side – they are usually laden with omega-6 oils – or you could scrap it altogether and dress it yourself with olive oil, vinegar, salt, pepper or chilli flakes. Your call.

MAIN COURSE

An easy principle is to go with the simplest sounding meal. The less complicated the dish, the better it is likely to be for you. For example, roasted chicken and grilled vegetables. It doesn't mean that your meal has to be boring; you can then mix it up yourself by adding interesting rainbow veggie side dishes and asking for extra chilli or herbs.

Look for menu options with the words grilled, poached, roasted, slow cooked and steamed. These cooking methods usually seal in the goodness and do not require being immersed in oils or sugary sauces.

Skip the dumb carb sides like French fries or white rice. Ask if they have a smarter carb alternative – they usually do.

DESSERT

If you have a nutritious, filling starter and a strong main course, then most of the time it's unlikely you will need a dessert and your body will feel satisfied. If you have ordered first, you may have already set the trend of a dessert pass. A digestive tea like camomile, peppermint or fennel is a good shout to finish off with something. Or if you really fancy something, opt for the cheese plate, or a fruit platter. Ask for just one scoop of ice cream rather than the usual three of a standard portion or share one with the table. All Ninja-agile tactics!

But sometimes, just order what you fancy. If your favourite cheese-cake is on the menu then have it and enjoy it. Remember, consistency beats intensity.

MEETINGS

Ideally, we shouldn't be in a meeting during our meal times, whether that be breakfast, lunch or dinner.

Make a stand and start to block out meal times in your calendar. Protect these precious moments, as they are essential to your success. However, we are also realistic and understand it may sometimes be completely out of your control. On these occasions, try to have some of the suggestions in this chapter prepped ahead; or, if you need to navigate a provided lunch, check out the Work Fuel guide to upgrading your choices opposite.

BUFFET LUNCH:

Avoid this	Upgrade to this
Fruit juices	Water/tea or vegetable juices
Crisps	Any salad or crudité option
Pastry items	Fruit platter
Beige or fried items – omega-6 nightmare	Cold meats/fish or cheese plates
Sandwich platter – basically eating lots of bread and little else	Make your sandwich a convertible! Throw the top away and add more veggies and protein to it – pick protein-rich fillings: egg, fish, chicken, cheese, hummus
Any pre-mixed dressings	Vinegar and olive oil

ON THE ROAD ALL WEEK

If you are on the road all week, then we appreciate it is tough, but it's not impossible to stick to the Work Fuel Way:

▶ Pack some of the options mentioned earlier in the 'Portables' section, at least for the start of the week.

▶ Get familiar with the local supermarket or grocery shop and buy some of the portables, so you can upgrade meals. Even a pack of cherry tomatoes added to an otherwise bland Caesar salad is a start.

▶ Get to know the better restaurants in the area – ask at the hotel, check apps such as Eatfit in the UK or Food Renegade in the US. They will recommend restaurants local to you with healthy options. If eating with others, take the lead and make the reservation for a better option than the fried-chicken place.

▶ Don't be afraid to order off-menu in restaurants if there aren't any options that work. The worst-case scenario is a refusal, but even then, there is usually a compromise. Just make sure you ask nicely.

Finally, perfection is the enemy of progress and you can't be spot on every time, especially when on the road. But what you can do each time is do the best you can with the options available. Consistency beats intensity.

EXERCISE: GETTING READY TO THRIVE

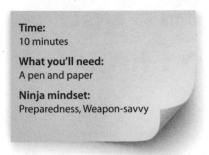

Time:
10 minutes

What you'll need:
A pen and paper

Ninja mindset:
Preparedness, Weapon-savvy

Step 1: Of the scenarios discussed in this chapter, which one do you experience most often?

- ▶ Air travel
- ▶ Hotel breakfasts
- ▶ Eating out
- ▶ Meetings
- ▶ On the road all week

Step 2: What one thing can you do to upgrade that scenario? Look back at that section for ideas and write it down.

Step 3: What do you need to buy/prepare to ensure this happens? For example, if it's a regular lunch meeting, can you ask in advance for Work Fuel lunch options? If you're on the road all week, what options can you add to your weekly food shop that you can take with you?

Are you a Ninja?

▶ A Ninja knows how to upgrade to the Work Fuel Way even when they're on the move or entering places that don't obviously support it. With a bit of preparedness, forward thinking and an attitude that 'there's usually a way', it's possible to sustain great habits just about anywhere.

▶ A Ninja loves the unorthodox: they'll happily eat their own food on the plane, go against the grain when booking a restaurant, or swap nuts for the biscuits provided in a meeting.

▶ All that said, consistency beats intensity, so the odd day where things don't quite go to plan is all part of the process – and a Ninja is human, not superhero, after all.

8.
HOW TO SHOP

There are three easy steps to shopping like a Ninja, ensuring you have a successful shop every time. It can be done virtually or physically. It will save your willpower, stop you from impulse buys, ensure you have real food in and maybe even a plan for what a week of meals could look like. You're going to want to start taking organization tips from your fridge!

THE THREE-STEP NINJA PROCESS

STEP 1: PREPAREDNESS

Throw away all those food-like substances lurking in your cupboards. Remember the eight key label-savvy principles (see pages 123–5) and just get rid of any that don't pass the test.

Do not use your willpower at home; there will be plenty of other places it is required. It may seem wasteful, but it's better in the bin than in your stomach.* If you keep these foods in the house, you *will* eat them at some point, usually when you are stressed and tired. All they will do is amplify these feelings. You eat good food if you have good food in.

---

* There are certain food items that foodbanks are always on the lookout for – for them, food that has a long shelf life is really helpful. Find your local bank and see if you can donate any of your unwanted items. While it's not going to provide you with optimum productivity, it can help someone in need.

EXERCISE: KITCHEN DETOX

Time:
Cupboard dependent

What you'll need:
You, your kitchen and an
uncompromising mind!

Ninja mindset:
Ruthlessness

Here's what needs to go:

Ditch	Switch
Processed and convenience foods	Actual ingredients to create meals with – see shopping list (pages 158–59)
Fizzy drinks – diet and non-diet varieties	Sparkling water – add in a slice of cucumber, lemon or lime, mint for flavour
Margarine	Extra virgin olive oil, butter, coconut butter
Milk chocolate	Dark chocolate, minimum 70% cocoa
Boxed breakfast cereals (we are hoping these have already left the building after Chapter 2 but here's a reminder just in case)	Porridge oats, chia seeds, nuts, seeds, low-sugar varieties of granola and muesli – be label-savvy
Table salt	Himalayan rock salt or sea salt – see note opposite
Pre-made salad dressings	Make your own – olive oil, lemon juice, salt, pepper, apple cider vinegar, mustard, fresh herbs
Flavoured yoghurts	Greek, natural yoghurt

A NOTE ON SALT

Not all salt is bad. In a study of 6,250 patients it was found that there was no actual link between salt intake, high blood pressure and risk of heart disease.[1] But it's important to differentiate between a natural salt and table salt. Table salt is mostly sodium chloride and is heavily processed. Natural salts come in their complete, whole form.

Worth their salt?

▶ **Natural sea salt** is typically much less refined than table salt, it contains many more beneficial minerals and tastes better to most people. However, in recent findings there have been suggestions that it may contain micro-plastics, something that is most definitely not Work Fuel.[2] The safest bet is pink Himalayan rock salt.

▶ **Pink Himalayan rock salt** is rich in minerals, containing all 84 essential trace elements required by your body. Pink salt can assist in many bodily functions, such as reducing muscle cramps, promoting blood sugar health and promoting healthy pH in your cells.[3]

STEP 2: PLAN

Before shopping, plan your meals for the week and create a list to shop from. It takes a few minutes, but saves time in store, stops impulse buys of processed foods, and ensures you have what you need. If you can devise a regular weekly list to return to, even better.

RETURN ON INVESTMENT MEAL PLAN

We have created a visual of how a working week may look with some of our suggested meals – see pages 152–7. We have shown two weeks, so you can start to visualize what prepping and having frozen meals ready to go may look like over a longer period of time. Perhaps you made curry two weeks ago and froze it. You know you need to work late tomorrow – defrost it in the fridge and you have dinner ready to go. It's a return on your previous investment, like a gift to your future self.

We have also included the required time investment needed. As suggested earlier, Sunday is a good day for this kind of prep, ahead of the week and without stress. Equally it could be Monday night or midweek – whenever you can schedule it in. Just ensure you do schedule it. Check your working week in advance – how many lunches/dinners out are expected? Any extra early starts or late finishes? Be kind to yourself on these days and prep in advance.

THE JOY OF BATCHING

Upgrading your habits often takes a huge additional investment of time. However, as you'll see, the great thing about batching your prep time is that the only thing that really changes is that you need to be slightly more organized and strategic. It doesn't actually take you any more time if you're already cooking a few meals and spending time popping out to stand in queues to buy sandwiches.

Of course, if all you eat now is toast, it may mean a slight increase in prep time, but your opportunity for improvement will be much greater too.

The timings are approximate: we don't know where your cooking skills are at – you could be the next Jamie Oliver or need supervision cutting an onion. So, it's going to vary; these are ideas for you to start to conceptualize how small the investment is versus the gains you will get in return.

Even if you *do* need to take a little more time ...

Let's make a comparison. We spend on average at least one hour twenty minutes per day on social media. That's nine hours twenty minutes per week. The result is you get to see what a guy you went to school with is doing on a beach in Malaysia, watch some crazy cat video or 'heart' a load of strangers' dinners on Instagram. Light relief perhaps, but it isn't going to feed you, it isn't going to nourish your brain, help you sleep better, give you the focus to complete that complex email or even get you that next new deal or role.[4]

We are talking around three hours per week prepping your fuel – could you scale back the smartphone use by just a third? What an amazing return; if you were a customer of such an offer in a business environment you would have already bought it in. This is your personal energy, well-being and productivity we are talking about here, so let's do it.

For all the dishes mentioned here, we have recipes in the back of the book – pages 215–34.

WEEK 1

	Sunday meal prep day (how long prepped item will keep)	Mon	Tues	
Breakfast	Overnight oats (see recipe page 79) (3 days) Time: 5 mins	Overnight oats with walnuts, apple, kefir & cinnamon	Overnight oats with walnuts, sunflower seeds, berries, kefir & cinnamon	
Lunch	Batch chopping salad items for the week (3–5 days) Roasting veg – sweet potatoes, aubergine, peppers, courgette (3–5 days) Boiled eggs (7 days) Time: 30 mins	Chopped salad with boiled egg & smoked salmon	Chopped salad with roasted veg, sauerkraut & feta	
Dinner	Batch cooking: Chilli Quinoa, whole bag (Portion and freeze) Time: 30 mins	Roasted veg with quinoa, feta & a sprinkle of seeds on top	Chilli with quinoa & avocado smash with smoked paprika	
Total investment time	65 minutes prep	15 minutes per day assembly	15 minutes per day assembly	

Weds	Thurs	Fri	Sat
Overnight oats with seeds, berries, kefir & cinnamon	1 or 2 slices of toast with avocado, tomato, 2 boiled eggs & chilli flakes	1 or 2 slices of toast with scrambled eggs, avocado, tomato, spinach, mushrooms	
Chopped salad with roasted veg, quinoa & mixed beans	Chopped salad with quinoa, falafel & hummus	Out for lunch. Follow the restaurant menu survival tactics on page 139	
Roasted veg with mackerel (vacuum packed), sauerkraut & beetroot	Chilli topped with grilled chicken or quinoa with seeds	Mix of whatever is left. Add in extra protein sources from freezer or larder	Total for week investment in Work Fuel
15 minutes per day assembly	15 minutes per day assembly	25 minutes per day assembly	2 hours 30 mins

WEEK 2

	Sunday meal prep day (how long prepped item will keep)	Mon	Tues	
Breakfast	Boiled eggs (7 days) Time: 6 mins	2 × boiled eggs with smashed avocado, sauerkraut & chilli with slice of sourdough toast	1 × boiled egg with cottage cheese with sourdough toast and beetroot & tomato	
Lunch	Batch chopping salad items for the week Time: 15 mins	Curry with rice & salad	Chopped salad with leftover fishcakes & quinoa (week 1)	
Dinner	Batch cooking: Curry Fishcakes Rice (Portion and freeze) Time: 60–75 minutes	Fishcakes with salad & fresh chilli	Dinner out: Follow the restaurant menu survival tactics on page 139	
Total investment time	95 minutes prep	15 minutes per day assembly	15 minutes per day assembly	

Weds	Thurs	Fri	Sat
Smoothie – make enough for 2 days	Smoothie	No time today: ½ an avocado with lime, rock salt & chilli; packed boiled egg	
Chopped salad with boiled egg, mackerel (vacuum packed) & horseradish	Out for lunch. Follow the restaurant menu survival tactics on page 139	Chopped salad with leftovers of hot smoked salmon frittata	
Curry with rice and veggies from freezer	Chopped salad with hot smoked salmon frittata	Chilli (from week 1, frozen in the meantime) with rice & avocado with yoghurt	Total for week investment in Work Fuel
15 minutes per day assembly	15 minutes per day assembly	25 minutes per day assembly	3 hours

While you may not be vegetarian or vegan, you may be interested in how to create Work Fuel meals without animal products. Here are some ideas:

VEGAN/VEGETARIAN OPTIONS

	Sunday meal prep day (how long prepped item will keep)	Mon	Tues	
Breakfast	Overnight oats (see recipe page 79) (3 days) Time: 5 minutes	Overnight oats with walnuts, apple, coconut kefir & cinnamon	Overnight oats with walnuts, sunflower seeds, berries, coconut kefir & cinnamon	
Lunch	Batch chopping salad items for the week (3–5 days) Roasting veg – sweet potatoes, aubergine, peppers, courgette (3–5 days) Time: 30 minutes	Chopped salad with falafel, beetroot & hummus	Chopped salad with roasted veg, topped with seeds and nuts	
Dinner	Batch cooking: Falafels Veggie curry Barley/quinoa/lentils once cooked, mix together or mix and match for meal assembly (Portion and freeze) Time: 75 minutes	Curry with lentils and rice	Falafel and lentil bowl reheated & topped with hummus and sauerkraut	
Total investment time	110 minutes prep	15 minutes per day assembly	15 minutes per day assembly	

Weds	Thurs	Fri	Sat
Overnight oats with almonds, pumpkin seeds, coconut kefir & kiwi	1 or 2 slices of toast with ½ tin of baked beans (low or no sugar variety), mushrooms, spinach & tomato	1 or slices of toast with ½ tin of baked beans (low or no sugar variety), mushrooms, spinach & tomato	
Chopped salad with lentils, roasted veg, beetroot & hummus	Roasted veg with barley, dukkah and ½ tin of chickpeas	Freestyle. Mix of whatever is left. Add in extra protein sources from freezer or larder	
Curry with barley & extra boiled/steamed veggies from freezer	Blend left-over roasted veggies & grains, add to veggie stock with herbs &/or curry powder	Dinner out: Follow the restaurant menu survival tactics on page 139	Total for week investment in Work Fuel
15 minutes per day assembly	15 minutes per day assembly	15 minutes per day assembly	3 hours 5 minutes

YOUR SHOPPING LIST

The list below is aligned to the Work Fuel Plate: protein, smarter carbs and rainbow foods. If you add a protein to your list, don't forget to add a rainbow and smarter carbs too, so your plate is complete.

Weekly Fridge Basics	Monthly Cupboard Basics	
Protein *Dairy and alternatives:* Milk. Cows, goat or plant (unsweetened) Greek, natural or plant yoghurt (🔋) Butter (organic if poss) Kefir (🔋) Feta cheese Jarlsberg (🔋) *Meat and fish:* Organic, grass-fed meat/poultry SMASH fish (vacuum packed) (🐟) Hot smoked salmon (🐟) Organic eggs *Rainbow plants* *Pre-packed foods:* Beetroot (vacuum packed) *Low-fructose fruits – what's in season:* Berries Kiwi Apples Avocados Lemons and limes *Veggies:* Dark leafy greens (🐟) Bagged salads Onions Tomatoes Peppers Cucumber Broccoli *Smarter carbs* *Bread:* Sourdough Rye	*Protein* *Tinned Fish:* Mackerel, anchovies, sardines (🐟) *Seeds and nuts:* Walnuts (🐟) Almonds Pumpkin (🐟) Sunflower Chia (🐟) *Rainbow plants* *Tins:* Tomatoes (chopped) Olives *Smarter carbs* *Tins:* Selection of beans – unsalted and no sugar (not baked): kidney, navy, pinto, black, fava, cannellini or mixed cans Coconut milk *Pre-cooked foods:* Brown rice/quinoa/lentils/barley *Teas/coffee:* Good-quality coffee – light roast Black tea Green tea Herbal teas (e.g. turmeric, ginseng, rooibos, peppermint, cinnamon for daytime; valerian, camomile, lime blossom, passionflower for night-time) *Fats:* Extra virgin olive oil Coconut oil Butter Nut butter (almond, peanut, hazelnut, cashew) *Jar foods:* Sauerkraut (🔋) Kombucha (🔋 – ensure you check the label for sugar levels, buy if 5 g or less per 100 ml) Kimchi (🔋) Roasted peppers Beans – same varieties as tinned, mentioned above	

We have also added in omega-3 (≈⊂⊃) foods and a good selection of fermented foods (▤), so you remember to include these on your lists.

Monthly Freezer Basics	Biannual Shop for Spices
Protein *Fish:* Salmon/mackerel fillets (≈⊂⊃) White fish fillets Prawns & shellfish *Meat:* Chicken breast fillets Lean steak mince **Rainbow plants** *Vegetables:* Peas Broccoli Spinach Peppers Onions Edamame beans *Fruits:* Berries Avocado *Herbs:* Ginger, garlic, coriander, cayenne, parsley, oregano, mint **Smarter carbs** *Bread:* Sourdough Rye	Himalayan rock salt Pepper Cayenne pepper Cumin Smoked paprika Ginger Turmeric Bay leaves Oregano Mixed Italian herbs Cinnamon Cacao (And some recommended powdered blends, to add heaps of flavour: Tikka masala Dukkah Korma Garam masala)

STEP 3: SHOP THE OUTSIDES

While in the supermarket, try to keep to the perimeter, shopping the outside aisles where fresh foods like fruit, vegetables, dairy, meat and fish are usually located. You'll find that the centre aisles are where the fake foods usually live. Only dip in for pre-planned items like tinned fish, beans, spices and dried goods.

> ● **REMEMBER THIS** ●
>
> Don't shop hungry. An empty stomach often results in crisp multipacks, biscuits and two-for-one purchases of pain au chocolat.

MAKE IT EVEN EASIER FOR YOURSELF

Online shopping
Create an online shop that you simply repeat. It may take half an hour to set up, but it saves heaps of time in the long run. Add everything from the weekly fridge basics and then create another 'big shop' list, where you add in the monthly cupboard basics too.

Monthly/bimonthly or weekly organic fruit and veg box
Value wise, these boxes work out to a comparable price to non-organic supermarket equivalents. Plus, they tend to be seasonal foods, and because the contents change regularly without your intervention, by design you are eating more varied and daring veggies. Oh, and you are more likely to eat more of it when it's there too. Check out Abel & Cole and Riverford in the UK or do a quick search for suppliers in your area.

EAT SEASONALLY, WHEN YOU CAN

It's worth mentioning that when we consume food that is aligned to the seasons, we are eating foods when they are at their peak taste, have higher nutritional content and are cheaper to buy. Check out these great websites that keep you up to date with food for the seasons, including recipes and where to buy: www.eattheseasons. co.uk and www.ewg.org

ORGANIC VS NON-ORGANIC

We think it makes good sense for you and the environment to choose organic when you can. Not only is it better for the planet, there is growing evidence that there are key health benefits to organic food. For example, research from Newcastle University suggests that both organic milk and meat contain around 50% more beneficial omega-3 fatty acids than conventionally produced products. You get more for your money.[5]

> • REMEMBER THIS •
>
> The Environmental Working Group (EWG) create a list each year called 'The Dirty Dozen and the Clean 15'. Strawberries topped the list in 2018 as the dirtiest, most sprayed crop with the highest levels of residual pesticides and herbicides. So, if you are going to buy any fruit or veg organic, strawberries are your number one, closely followed by spinach, nectarines, apples and grapes. On the flip side, avocados topped the 2018 list of the 'Clean 15'. It's a naturally resistant crop and has little or negligible levels of these chemicals. Save your money, buy regular avocados – they are pricey enough as it is. The same goes for sweetcorn, pineapple, cabbages and onion.
>
> To check out the most recent version go to: **www.ewg.org**

WHAT ABOUT SUPPLEMENTS ON OUR SHOPPING LIST?

The key here is the name: 'supplement'. They can enhance a balanced diet, but not replace it. They supplement something that is already good; the foundation is always eating real food. There is no magic pill.

Most of us will have taken supplements at some point, because we read an article about how they boost this or that. Often people are taking multiple supplements and can't even remember why. Sometimes there is a sense of total bewilderment and confusion over what to take. At best they may be expensive pee, at worst you might be building up toxic levels of something.

However, even with a balanced diet there's potential for deficiency and this is where supplements do add value. This is due to:

1. Modern farming practices – the soil just isn't what it was, so minerals such as magnesium are found in lower levels.

2. We live more stressful lives than ever before, so are in need of more nutrients. Being under a lot of stress can deplete many nutrients including calcium, magnesium and zinc, as these are used to help the body cope with stressful situations. Stress can also reduce digestive strength (as we know from the lion in our lunch break in Chapter 4). This, in turn, reduces nutrient absorption and utilization even further.[6]

What about supplements with their own jingle?

You tend to get what you pay for with supplements – a supermarket-sourced fish oil will be very different therapeutically than one sourced from a specialist in the market. Some, such as those fizzy absorbing ones, have a lot of caffeine and additives. There's a lot of marketing blurb about these products now too – even jingles – so please remember what we advise about those! Don't be fooled into thinking you can't function without this or that. However, there are certainly benefits to a more individual level of targeted supplementation. Rather than us giving you blanket information that simply isn't going to be applicable to everyone, our advice is if you do decide to supplement your diet, do your research, don't overdose (which can be harmful), seek advice from an expert and buy the best you can afford.

Are you a Ninja?

▶ A Ninja adopts the mentality of 'batch processing' to minimize prep time.

▶ A Ninja gets into a rhythm in the way that they shop, buying herbs and spices in bulk, having great weekly and monthly lists for online shopping, and using a veg box service to keep them on their toes with seasonal vegetables.

▶ A Ninja knows that certain foods are much better if they're bought organic, but that other foods don't need to be the pricey organic options to be nutriful and free of chemical nasties.

9.
THE TOOLKIT

TOOLS **FOR THE JOB**

There's often more to eating well than just the food, or even the shopping. So here's a bunch of things that we think will make your life easier: at

'We are what we repeatedly do. Excellence, therefore, is not an act, but a habit.'
– Aristotle

home in the kitchen, to carry around in your work bag or leave in your desk, and a few other things that can help promote the Work Fuel Way.

HOME KITCHEN

We've kept equipment simple. You may already have it, but we thought it was best not to assume. Here are the kitchen basics:

- ▶ A set of saucepans, including a casserole pan

- ▶ Non-stick frying pan – oven proof if possible, so no plastic handles

- ▶ Chopping board

- ▶ A decent set of knives

- ▶ Vegetable peeler

- ▶ Spatula

- ▶ A selection of Tupperware. Glass is great, but heavier to carry, so look for BPA-free plastic options for prepped lunches, nextovers and batch cooking. Some containers are free of charge: don't throw away empty jars – reuse and repurpose

- ▶ Roasting tray; have a few of these – always useful

▶ A blender. This can be a cheap stick blender, a bullet-type container model (less washing up as you drink from the same container you blended in) or an extravagant-as-you-like food processer. This is an area worth investing in, as you can make so much in them: smoothies, dips, soups – even your own peanut butter. Colette's blender cost more than her first car, but eight years in, it's still going strong, is used most days and is never off her kitchen countertop – the cost per use now is probably similar to a pair of socks! Plus it makes a hot soup from raw ingredients in just seven minutes. Check out **www.workfuel. ninja/blenders** for our favourites

▶ Kitchen scales

▶ Measuring jug.

A FEW OPTIONAL CONSIDERATIONS:

▶ A non-stick muffin tray (to be used for the savoury variety)

▶ A salad spinner – it really does transform the crunchiness of salads and extends shelf life

▶ A box grater (collects the grated food underneath, less mess and a storage box too)

▶ A slow cooker. You place all the ingredients from our curry, soup or chilli recipes in it and turn it on – job done.

WORK BAG

A few essentials for when you are on the go:

BYO cutlery: Picking up plastic throwaway cutlery every day is morally bankrupt, and despite Colette's best efforts, business cards just aren't a suitable knife replacement. In the UK, we use disposable plastic forks on average for just three minutes before we throw them away! This stuff takes millennia to break down. Just BYO.[1]

Sustained energy in packets: Pumpkin seeds, sunflower seeds, any raw nuts, if pushed could replace a meal.

Glass or metal water bottle.

OFFICE *TOOLKIT*

If feasible, you can transform your desk drawer or locker into a mini kitchen storage area. Include:

▶ Mini chopping board

▶ A proper knife

▶ Small salad spinner

▶ Tin opener

▶ Tinned fish (sardines, mackerel and tuna)

▶ Tinned beans (butter, cannellini, kidney, etc.)

▶ Selection of herbs and spices (rosemary, sage, cayenne, paprika)

▶ Nuts

▶ Seeds

▶ Olive oil.

KEEPING A FOOD DIARY

If you tried to recall everything you ate and drank yesterday, chances are you'd forget a thing or two (or five). We tend to interpret what we ate in a more positive light. Cornell University researchers used a hidden camera to spy on diners at an Italian restaurant. Just five minutes after the meal was over, they asked diners how much bread they had consumed. Most people had eaten about 30% more than they thought, and 12% of people who were seen eating bread on camera denied having had any at all.[2]

Keeping a diary for a couple of weeks will give you a greater insight into your actual eating behaviour and energy. It will answer questions like:

▶ Why you eat when not hungry

▶ How much you really eat of certain foods

▶ How you feel after eating certain foods.

It also helps to outline where you can make the biggest investments and where to start. You could use a physical record or note everything down in an app like MyFitnessPal or Pinto. We have a diary template online at **www.workfuel.ninja/diary** which you can download, print and fill in. It is also helpful to note down the times of day that you are eating, in case you see any revealing patterns.

ARE SOME FOODS *DISTRESSING YOU WITHOUT YOU NOTICING?*

A food diary is also a great tool to spot patterns and correlate certain foods with how they make you feel. If you are being adversely affected by food it can be energy draining, and if you are unknowingly eating food that you are intolerant to it can make you feel very unwell. If you notice a pattern, it's worth investigating further, eliminating that food and speaking to your GP or a registered/qualified nutritionist who can offer further advice.

IS THERE *AN APP FOR THAT?*

We are going to talk in the next two chapters about lifestyle and forming habits. These are areas where an app can be helpful. We've both been big users of Fitbit and some of the other apps and smart watches, in particular the apps' ability to track things like daily steps, heart rate and sleep. While neither of us use the food tracker any more (it just feels like second nature to eat well now), it's a great way to keep a food diary if you're on the move. Likewise, more dedicated apps like MyFitnessPal and Pinto will also help to encourage mindfulness at mealtimes (because you know you have to tell the app exactly what you've eaten!).

If you don't fancy making a detailed diary entry every day, you can use an app like Streaks (iPhone) or HabitBull (Android) to provide questions or gentle remind-ers to yourself, and even create geeky little graphs to track your progress. Of course, you can get really detailed if you want to, but adding a simple question to one of these apps to say 'Did I eat the rainbow today?' or 'Remember the Work Fuel Plate' is all you need.

A FEW ALTERNATIVES – GET WEIRD!

There are a few additional tools that you could experiment with. They are not usually found in productivity books, or nutrition ones, or even in work bags, but they may just give us another edge. Unorthodoxy is the way of the Ninja.

THE POWER OF SMELL

Smell is perhaps not a subject to which many of us give much thought, but evidence suggests it can in fact have an enormous impact on productivity. This is partly due to the receptors in our noses communicating with parts of our brain that process emotion and learning.

ESSENTIAL 'PRODUCTIVITY' OILS

Inhaling essential oils activates the hypothalamus, an area of the brain which sends messages to other parts of the body. Try a few drops of these on a cotton wool ball or tissue – a sleeve even – whenever you need their effect, or use a diffuser at home.

Lemon = Concentration. Helpful when feeling angry, anxious or run down and when you need to focus. A study in Japan by Takasago Corporation found that 54% of typists made fewer errors when they could smell lemon, 33% made fewer with jasmine and 20% made fewer with lavender. It also has antiviral and antibacterial properties, great for when on public transport![3]

Rosemary = Pick me up. In addition to improving memory retention, rosemary has stimulating properties that fight physical exhaustion, headaches and mental fatigue.[4]

Peppermint = Energy boost. Try peppermint when brainstorming – it helps to invigorate the mind, promotes concentration and stimulates clear thinking.[5]

Lavender = Calm. Known for having a soothing effect on the nerves and mood and can relieve nervous tension.[6] In the same Japanese study by the Takasago Corporation, mentioned above, it was found that lavender and rosemary noticeably decrease the stress hormone cortisol.

● REMEMBER THIS ●

When travelling, Colette always carries some lavender essential oil. It helps to refresh hotel rooms and gives a bit of calm in the security queue – just a few drops on the wrist and inhale.

GET GREEN

Get your own plant buddy on your desk at work or at home. This has been shown to boost productivity and creativity by as much as 15%. There is a theory that suggests that by just looking at nature the brain shifts into a different processing mode, making individuals feel more relaxed and better able to concentrate. Peace lilies, snake plants and money plants are low maintenance and great air conditioners.[7]

ADAPTOGENIC HERBS

On social media these foods are having their heyday. Adaptogens are plants that are proposed to increase our resistance to stress, helping our bodies to adapt and adjust. For example, they may help calm us in times of stress or they may give energy when we are tired. There are many; we have chosen just three that you can buy in a powder form, available in health stores, some supermarkets and via online retailers. These can then be added to your morning smoothie or sprinkled on top of foods. Use as advised on packaging.

Ashwagandha: Known as a cortisol (stress hormone) balancer, this may support the body during stressful periods. It's a powerful herb to have on hand, as it has been shown to reduce anxiety by up to 44%.[8]

Maca: Clinical trials have shown that maca may positively impact energy and stamina. Maintaining positive energy levels can also help improve mood and some early studies have even found that maca may reduce symptoms of depression.[9]

Reishi: This mushroom helps boost mental clarity and lower blood sugar levels. It's also an anti-inflammatory, associated with enhanced longevity and immunity.[10]

Are you a Ninja?

▶ A Ninja knows that good kit often means good outcomes. With the right pots and pans and a few extras, you're better set up for success – which you can track and celebrate, using an app.

▶ A Ninja is prepared and squirrels away items in their desk, such as cutlery, olive oil and, of course, nuts and seeds.

▶ A Ninja loves unorthodoxy and isn't afraid to throw a few bits of weirdness in here and there, whether it's essential oils, pot plants or maca powder. If it works, it works.

10.
LIFESTYLE

OF COURSE, IT'S NOT ALL ABOUT EATING

We've taken you through a myriad of ways to improve your attention and energy with food. Of course, if practised in isolation, these principles will be useful and healthy, but they will only get you so far. Someone eating the best diet but then substituting four hours of their sleep time for red wine time is unlikely to be feeling wonderful the next day. In this chapter, we'll be looking at some of the other factors that drive the energy for great productivity. Sleep, exercise, good Productivity Ninja habits, our mental health, social life, taking breaks, meditation and many other factors all contribute to how we feel. We're going to touch on a few key principles, but without  trying to cover all the bases. There's simply too much to squeeze all these topics in properly. So, if you were wondering, that's why this book isn't called 'the holistic guide to everything you should do for a perfect life'.

HOLISTIC BUT NOT 'EVERYTHING'

How did that alternative book title make you feel? *Everything* you *should* do for a *perfect* life. This is something we think needs addressing: the Instagram effect. We are now living in an age seemingly more obsessed with self-care – and most certainly with 'self' – than ever before. This can be a positive thing. We're often inspired by a nice catchy quote or a reminder that there are practical steps we can take to get better at stuff. The downside is that it can reach a saturation point where each inspirational quote loses its meaning. You can have too much of a good thing. You can become confused by conflicting advice or just numbed by the constant push for perfection.

So, while we talk about these useful things to do, don't try to change your whole life overnight either. If you're trying to focus on everything, you're ultimately focused on nothing.

Give yourself a break. You're doing great. You are enough. So many 'gurus' and 'thought-leaders' will tell you *everything* should be optimized: hack your bodies, hack your minds, download this software, drink these special potions, learn how to optimize everything from your empathy to your light switches. We think it's dangerous once you head too far down that road. You can't always do everything. Get comfortable with imperfection. Know that there's always something that you won't get right, or you might wish was different. Tackling your life and productivity holistically is one thing but beating yourself up trying to get everything perfect is a recipe for demotivation.

It's so tempting to sit there at Christmas or on holiday and dream up the ideal daily routines. You've probably done similar ones. They all go something along the lines of: get up, exercise before breakfast, have time for a great breakfast, meditate, do some quiet reading, listen to jazz, do yoga, 'thinking time' spent walking in the countryside … and that's all on a Monday. The truth is most of these routines last no more than a couple of weeks. Once the smug excitement of the routine wears off, you lose motivation, and something called life usually gets in the way. We both do many of these things during an average week, but we'd say we both probably do them all more often now that it's more free-form, and we've stopped trying to live the perfect day.

GOOD PRODUCTIVITY HABITS

People often think of work as something that 'takes its toll' on your energy or well-being. But developing positive productivity habits in your working life can actually be good for you, releasing happiness chemicals like dopamine in the brain and increasing motivation towards other positive habits, because success breeds success – dopamine is literally addictive. But what constitute good productivity habits? Here are some of the key building blocks, based on a few key points from Graham's book *How to be a Productivity Ninja*:

▶ Aim to regularly experience **Zen-like calm** by getting all ideas, nags or potential actions out of your head and manage them all in a 'second brain' (an app or paper-based system that sets out your projects and actions, so that you have a clear idea of your commitments).

▶ Use some **Ninja ruthlessness** to keep your email inbox at zero – because the magic happens when you feel able to get outside of your email.

▶ Practise **stealth and camouflage** by making yourself deliberately less available, so that you can get some work done, away from the noisy world of the internet or the open-plan office.

▶ Take the **unorthodox** route sometimes, such as cutting down on social media, or removing certain apps from your phone. Beat procrastination by deciding things by dice, or suggesting stand-up meetings to save time.

▶ Recognize the fact that **we're human** and our brains can sometimes derail us – in particular, notice those times when our 'lizard brain' (the primitive part of the brain that gives us 'fight or flight' syndrome and controls our basic survival instincts) tries to stop us from taking risks or dealing with necessary conflicts or difficulties because it craves comfort and safety.

▶ Getting really good at the four key productivity habits: capturing and collecting information; organizing everything by projects and next physical actions; reviewing your second brain thoroughly each week and briefly each day; and focusing on 'do' habits to avoid resistance and keep yourself in a state of productive flow.

MEDITATION

One of the other Productivity Ninja characteristics is mindfulness. By now, it seems everyone has heard about the many benefits of meditation. Apps such as Headspace, Calm, Buddhify and Insight Timer all help take a habit that can initially be quite difficult to adopt and make it something accessible, easy to develop and even share with others.

So why are meditation and other forms of mindfulness practice so useful for our productivity and for our mental health? Ultimately, it's because meditation allows us to practise putting our focus on one thing (for example our breathing) and our brain changes state, which acts like a mental refresh. But there are other ways to achieve the same results, if straight meditation feels too hard or too annoying at first, try a different approach. Here are five options:

1. Yoga. We are huge fans of yoga as a mindfulness practice, and it brings many other benefits such cardio fitness, better joint and muscle health, flexibility (thanks to yoga, Graham can touch his toes for the first time in years!) and much more. The same can be said for similar practices like Pilates or tai chi. If you haven't tried it, you are missing out. There are styles to suit almost anyone, so don't dismiss it with just one class. If you want a dynamic cardio workout, try vinyasa flow or power yoga. If you would like to try a softer style, look out for yin yoga, hatha yoga or yoga nidra – the last one is great for sleep.

2. Walking. Have you noticed how spending a few minutes walking mindfully in the park, taking time to notice your surroundings, your breathing and how your mind races, is never something you regret doing afterwards? So often we tell ourselves we don't have time for such things, but they clear the mind and we always thank ourselves afterwards. In Japan this has been known for a while as *shirin-yoku*, literally 'forest bath'. There is now a book with the same title and numerous studies demonstrating its effects, which include a measurable reduction in anxiety, depression and cortisol levels.[1]

   > 'Mindfulness means paying attention in a particular way: on purpose, in the present moment, and non-judgmentally.'
   > – Jon Kabat-Zinn

3. Centring (and other embodiment practices). Centring is a simple technique where you mentally scan and draw focus through the 'centre' of the body, relaxing your forehead, face, tongue, neck, shoulders and stomach muscles. It takes a few seconds to do but draws your mind back to your body as well as back to the present moment. It's a great thing to do in queues, on the train, or while you wait for the printer to finish in the office. If you've

never tried it before, there's a great app simply called 'centring', which guides you through the process.

4. Mindful eating. When was the last time you sat down to eat, on your own, with no screen in front of you? Eating mindfully, with your focus fully on every mouthful and every chew, is not only great for the digestive process, but it's a brilliant way to approach something we're going to do anyway as a mindfulness practice.

5. Journalling. Whether it's a daily diary, a gratitude journal or a practice like Julia Cameron's 'morning pages' technique (where you write three full pages of your stream of consciousness first thing in the morning), there's something empowering about using writing to listen to your thoughts. Apps like Bliss can make gratitude journalling accessible as something to do at any moment of the day, and it's a much better way to fill a journey than with Candy Crush.

EXERCISE

Mixing exercise with work can be tricky, especially if you work in an office with no access to showers and the like. Being able to exercise in short bursts can help you fit in the fitness.

HIIT

High-intensity interval training, or HIIT[2] for short, has been found to be a particularly good way to boost brain function. Studies have found it can increase endorphins, thereby increasing motivation to exercise, as well as increase mitochondrial function, which is a marker of your cells' ability to produce energy. You can find a plethora of HIIT workouts on YouTube to 'play along' to. Joe Wicks has become the YouTube master when it comes to HIIT, and we are fans of his workouts. The clue's in the name, and HIIT is an intense form of exercise, which you should only approach from a reasonable starting level of fitness, but one of the best things about it is that it's over in no more than fifteen minutes.

> ● REMEMBER THIS ●
>
> A short burst of running can also have positive effects. A Stanford University study found that even just fifteen minutes of running can improve energy, memory and brain function.[3] Simply running home from the school after dropping off the kids, or replacing a commuter train with a run can make it an integral part of your day, rather than it becoming just another thing you need to find time to do.

STANDING DESKS AND MOVING AT WORK

You've probably heard the phrase that 'sitting is the new smoking'. While it's true that standing at your desk (and Graham is standing up right now as he types these words!) is generally found to be better, it's not as clear-cut as you think. The worst choice you can make is sitting all day, but the real benefits of using a standing desk happen when you combine them with other forms of exercise too. Simply put, standing helps us move, and moving helps us think. How can you create more movement at work? Write down a few options now. For example: take the stairs everyday, instead of the lift. Schedule more walk-and-talk meetings, or perhaps walk across the office to speak to your colleagues in person rather than over email.

SLEEP

Arianna Huffington's book *The Sleep Revolution* has begun to draw attention to what she calls the 'collective delusion that overwork and burnout are the price we must pay to succeed'. Good energy comes from good sleep. Never see sleep as a luxury, it's a biological necessity. And if you feel guilty about going to bed early – or even on time! – when things are busy, then train your brain to see sleep as simply one more way of practising Ninja preparedness. Lions prepare for the hunt by sleeping. A lot.

Sleep hygiene is a vital area, made more difficult by our addiction to technology. Get into the habit of charging your devices away from the bedroom, so that you have some quality wind-down time before bed. Set reminders on your phone saying, 'Put me away now!' if you need to. Use apps like Twilight to reduce the blue light from your screen as the sun goes down, so that you feel less 'wired'. Be screen-free for the last hour before bed. And if you're sitting reading this thinking 'but I use my phone as an alarm clock!' then we have a radical piece of advice for you. Buy an alarm clock. They're really cheap these days. Keep a regular time for bed, and learn how long you need to sleep. The experts say it's a minimum of seven hours and no more than nine hours. Where are you on this scale? It's worth working this out and then sticking to it.

Sleep becomes even more vital when you have smaller members of the family who seem to enjoy waking you up too early or keeping you up half the night. If it's possible, try to adjust your sleep schedule to start earlier to fall more into line with your kids. And never – ever – feel guilty about taking a nap during the day when you need to. Think of a nap as vital Ninja preparedness instead of lost time.

VITAMIN D IS IN THE SKY

Of course, food isn't the only place to get vitamins and minerals. Vitamin D is absorbed through the skin, particularly when areas that are not always exposed, such as the chest or trunk, are in sunlight. In the UK and similar climates, the advice is that winter sunshine won't contain enough UVB radiation to produce vitamin D, so we're more reliant on food or supplements to produce it, but anything that says lying around in the summer sunshine is good for your health has to be encouraged, we think (with a good sunscreen on, of course!).

The sun and sky are also important when you're travelling and want to reduce the effects of jet lag.[4] Your body clock is rooted in the suprachiasmatic nucleus of the hypothalamus, which sits just behind the eyes. Exposure to sunlight is what tells the brain 'it's daytime' or 'it's night-time'. So, when you arrive somewhere and it's the middle of the day, and all you want to do is sleep, the mere act of walking around in the sunshine will help your body reset its clock to its new time zone. Likewise, when it's time to go to bed, make it as dark as possible so that the brain recalibrates to the new night-time as well.

Another tip for jet lag, alongside sunlight exposure and movement, is hydrotherapy. It may sound fancy, but put simply it's moving the dial from hot to cold in the shower a few times. The coldest you can manage for a few seconds and then back to warm, and repeat. This kick-starts the lymphatic system in the body and has a revitalizing effect.

ALCOHOL

Alcohol can derail even the most devoted of us. It causes massive blood sugar highs and lows, which makes you hungrier than usual (it isn't a coincidence the kebab shops are close to the pubs and bars!). Add in the bad foods, tiredness and dehydration with all that blood sugar fluctuation and you can see why alcohol knocks your focus; in fact, 11% of the sugar consumed in the UK is from alcohol. A pint of cider is the equivalent of eating a donut's worth of sugar; a large glass of wine is the same as a chocolate-covered ice cream cone – yet it would be difficult to eat five of these in row (for most of us at least).[5]

There is evidence to show that small amounts of alcohol, particularly red wine, may be helpful in protecting against heart disease and cognitive decline, so it's not all bad news, but excessive consumption clouds the mind and impairs your ability to think clearly.

WISER CONSUMPTION:

If you are going to be in an alcohol-fuelled environment, then here are some wise ideas for you:

▶ Choose naturally lower sugar options, such as white spirits with soda water and lime. Avoid any drinks that are pre-mixed, as these tend to be high in sugar and/or artificial sweeteners and possibly other additives, as well as chemical ingredients.

▶ Try a fake round, when out with friends. Choose an 'alcohol looking' option: fizzy water and a slice of lemon looks like a gin and tonic, for example. Sometimes it's just about having something in your hand. Graham is a big fan of real ales, but when he's cutting out alcohol, he'll buy two bottles of alcohol-free beer in the pub and pour them into a pint glass. His friends are none the wiser.

▶ Alternate each alcoholic drink with a glass of water. This helps keep you hydrated and clear-headed, so you can keep track of how much you're drinking.

▶ Never drink on an empty stomach. Food helps slow down the rate at which your body absorbs alcohol, meaning glucose production isn't affected as dramatically.

For more advice, support and information, check out www.drink aware.com

EXERCISE: STOP, START, CONTINUE

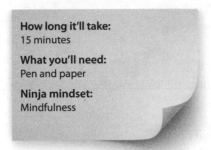

How long it'll take:
15 minutes

What you'll need:
Pen and paper

Ninja mindset:
Mindfulness

What has stood out the most for you in this chapter? That's your place to start. Think about that topic and write down:

Stop – What do you need to stop doing right now?

Start – Being specific, realistic and measured, what can you start today?

Continue – What's already going well?

Are you a Ninja?

▶ A Ninja knows good productivity means feeling less busy – which means you're more likely to make time for the right foods, which drive good productivity habits. It's a virtuous circle of momentum.

▶ A Ninja knows that beyond food, things like exercise and well-being will increase our agility. We don't need to spend hours in the gym to stay healthy, but we do need to make some effort.

▶ A Ninja knows that good sleep and preparedness are essential to brain function. Getting the right rest – and setting up our food habits to support good sleep – are fundamental aspects of performance.

11.

MAKING IT STICK: HABITS AND HOW TO STAY ON TRACK

One thing that is often missing from books about healthier eating is a focus on the process of creating and sustaining habits. It's something that we somewhat take for granted and assume that we know how to do – despite all the evidence to the contrary. In this chapter, we're going to look at how to set up a habit and get motivated, how to turn new behaviours into long-term habits, and what to do when you get stuck or things don't go to plan.

KNOWING OURSELVES

Let's start with a little peek into the depths of the soul. Understanding some key aspects of human psychology will help us set up changes that are sustainable and hopefully help you rocket-fuel your brain for years to come. There are some key elements to making any change:

- motivation
- willpower
- habit design
- turning the conscious change into unconscious routine.

MOTIVATION

What motivates you? In the case of this book, we hope that your motivation to eat well is driven by the promise of more energy and brain power. There may be more to it, but we're pretty explicit that that's our aim in sharing this book with you. But what motivates you in your choices in life?

INTRINSIC VS EXTRINSIC MOTIVATIONS

In particular, it's worth exploring the dynamics of intrinsic and extrinsic motivation. Intrinsic motivation comes from within. You do a thing because you want to, and you'd probably still do it if no one was ever going to find out. You learn to play the piano because you enjoy the music you create and value the challenge of self-improvement and mastery. If you're extrinsically motivated, you may be learning piano too, but probably because you're keen to get your grade 5 certificate, or you have a belief that getting good at piano means you can be as cool as Elton John or Ben Folds. Extrinsic motivation is about the external rewards. It's about what the rest of society thinks of you. It's about status, glory and acceptance in the tribe. When we start a project at work because we passionately believe in what we're doing, that's intrinsic motivation. When we have a project to do because our boss has given us a deadline, a target, or the motivation of a bonus or reward, then that's extrinsic motivation. Research generally points to intrinsic motivation as being more important for long-term success or sustained positive behaviour. But of course, all of us are motivated by different things at different times.

Neither is right or wrong, but understanding where we need a little push from others, or a little external reward, is important self-awareness. The trick is to constantly ask 'why'. Why do you want to make these changes? Is it really all about eating for brain power, or does part of you want to make these changes to impress someone, or be something? One of the useful things about understanding extrinsic motivation is that it gives you accountability. For example, if you want to give up a bad habit like smoking, it can help to say to your best friend or your partner, 'this is my last cigarette'. Whether you want to impress them, or just avoid that embarrassing feeling of losing face, that extrinsic motivation will help you to build day after day of not smoking – and the longer you continue that run of motivation, the closer you are to forming a new positive habit in its place.

WILLPOWER

The psychologist Roy Baumeister is famed for his research on self-control and willpower. Baumeister's work has helped us understand decision fatigue and the feeling of cognitive overload we feel when we're dealing with too many thoughts and choices. He coined the term 'ego depletion' to describe how each tiny decision – from choosing what to wear each morning to each email we read, what we choose to eat, and everything in between – slowly uses up our mental energy.

When it comes to food, we are often swerving between what we know is better for us and what we crave. Our bodies become trained to crave what they're regularly fed, and the Western palate is geared towards overly salty or overly sweet food choices. So, every time we consciously make the healthier choice, we are gradually using up a bit more of our mental energy. What Baumeister's work does is show us why this happens. Our self-control is gradually used up as we go through the day, like water being taken from a well, and then by sleeping and resting, we refill the well. So, our self-control and willpower is a depleting resource.

We can also think of self-control as a muscle: you wear it out if you overuse it, but with regular exercise, it can also be strengthened. His studies have found that practising self-control over one area of your life can give you extra reserves to call upon in other areas. So, if you become the master of getting out of bed in the morning, over time you have fewer things to resist, and more self-control left to master your diet or your to-do list. The positive momentum spills over from one area of life into another. It's all about gradually building up those daily reserves and not trying to change everything at once. This is why it's much easier to eat healthily if you're on a yoga retreat and not working for a week than it is in a normal working routine.

WILLPOWER IS OVERRATED

For this reason, relying on willpower to stay on track is a fool's errand, particularly if you need to 'spend' some of that self-control energy on other areas of your life, like not procrastinating, or choosing the gym over the pub on a Tuesday evening. What this leads us to is two things:

▶ The need to reduce the shock of the change (or put another way, make the change as easy as possible)

▶ The need to fully understand ourselves, so that we are using the right carrots and the right sticks to motivate us when we need a push (and are in tune with ourselves when our intrinsic motivation doesn't need support).

It's not enough to simply decide a new habit will be formed. We need to design the habit itself in advance. And in doing so we have the best opportunity to spot the crunch moments of weakness, and plan for success.

HABIT DESIGN

Charles Duhigg, author of *The Power of Habit*, breaks down a lot of the science of habit formation, and has identified that every habit has three important stages:

1. The cue – the moment in which our brain knows that a particular behaviour will follow

2. The routine – the behaviour itself

3. The reward – where our brain receives the reward for the behaviour.

For example, if we are talking about developing a running habit, the cue might be waking up and seeing our trainers set up next to the bed. That's the cue to put them on and run. The routine is the running itself. The reward, when we return, might be that we sit down and eat breakfast, or it might be that sweaty warm glow and rush of endorphins. We suddenly feel good because we exercised. Duhigg argues that when designing habits, too much attention is placed on the routine, whereas the brain needs clearer cues and clearer rewards to help entrench the habit. He even suggests making the rewards clearer by following difficult tasks or exercise with something pleasurable like chocolate (we'd suggest dark chocolate!) or a relaxing bath at the end of the day, so that we give our brains the most obvious instructions possible. This motivates us so that the cue stage becomes easier each day, which uses less willpower and eventually creates lasting habits.

TURNING CONSCIOUS INTO UNCONSCIOUS

In Chapter 1, we talked about the four stages of competence and how learning new habits or skills is a journey from unconscious incompetence (with food this might be simply not knowing what's good to eat), through to conscious incompetence (feeling guilty because we're making the wrong choices or realizing we're sluggish because of certain foods), through to conscious competence (knowing what we're doing – and succeeding – but it's taking up a lot of willpower and effort) to finally reaching the nirvana of unconscious competence (eating well, habitually, without even having to give these things much thought at all).

What's clear is that in designing habits, we need to focus on the jump from conscious competence to unconscious competence. Rest assured that while you will need to focus some energy on making some of these changes, it gets easier over time. Conscious choice is something our brains can rationalize and therefore argue with, creating more conflict and possible derailing, whereas habitual behaviour doesn't wake up the self-sabotaging aspects of the brain. The positive momentum and rewards from eating to fuel your brain rather than eating to follow your cravings will eventually create new and better cravings. When you crave healthy food, it finally becomes something you don't need to waste any willpower on. This is why working on creating habits rather than simply on creating motivation is so much more powerful.

GETTING GOING: CREATING HABITS THAT WORK

'Knowing is not enough;
we must apply. Willing is
not enough; we must do.'
– Johann Wolfgang von Goethe

The longer we spend anticipating the potential moments of weakness and understanding mindfully who we are and what motivates us, the more likely it is that our new habits will be successful. So what follows are the seven essential elements of good habit design. Spend some time reflecting on what you want, why you want it and how, practically, you can make it work for you (alongside everything else you've got going on in your life). And while we're using these seven elements here in relation to food choices, you can use this same model to help you get physically fit, write that novel, or stop looking at your phone too much.

THE 7 HABITS OF HIGHLY SUCCESSFUL HABIT DESIGN

1. Cues and rewards

Let's start with designing the right cues and rewards, as Charles Duhigg suggests. A cue is the moment that your brain recognizes that the positive behaviour begins. Duhigg talks about five types of cue:

- Time (e.g. we develop a morning routine or set an alarm to take a 3pm meditation break each day)

- Location (e.g. putting water on your desk to support staying hydrated or removing the biscuits from the cupboard next to where you make tea)

- Emotional (e.g. feeling happy about hitting a sales target and sharing it with the team, or noticing we're stressed and leaving the room)

- Other people (e.g. we choose a non-alcoholic drink because our friend does the same, or we go on a fitness routine because we're inspired by our boss having lost weight)

- The last event (e.g. we check our phone because it buzzes, or we cook more food with vegetables because we ordered a 'veg box' to be delivered).

For each habit that you want to develop, whether it's eating a great breakfast or getting into a good Ninja preparedness routine with your food shop, think of at least one of the above types of cue, and think about how the new habit you're designing should best be triggered. What can you do to put yourself in the place where the easiest possible thing is to do the thing you want to do?

Then, make sure you know what the reward is going to be. Here are a few ideas for how you can reward yourself:

- Buy yourself little feel-good luxuries like a new notepad or the kind of bath salts or aftershave you're only supposed to receive as gifts

- Save up the Netflix specials and rather than just watching them, make them conditional on you building your new habits

▶ At the end of a month, buy yourself tickets to a gig or theatre event

▶ The fancy tea bags

▶ A hug from someone you love.

Remember, what's important here is creating a signifier to the brain that says 'here's where I start the new habit, and here's the good stuff that happens as a result'. After a while, you won't need the reward, or you can shift the reward to be for something new. You don't have to stockpile bath salts in your house, but you do need something so obvious that the brain is left in no doubt: see reward; go get reward.

2. If/then behaviour chains

We are trying to make habits as easy as possible to form. Therefore, it's much easier to build new habits on top of existing habits than to create something completely from scratch. For each habit, think about where it fits into your everyday routines. It's helpful to think of this as an 'if/then' scenario:

If (or when) ...	Then ...
I'm out of the office buying lunch	I'll choose a healthier option by going to a healthier salad takeaway instead of the fast-food place
I'm home for the evening	I'll put my keys on the table, take my coat off, and quickly prepare my lunch for tomorrow (before I collapse on the sofa)
I'm out at a conference or event where I know the food options are not nutriful.	I'll buy something healthier on the way there or prepare something at home.

As you can see, a little bit of Ninja preparedness goes a long way. What we're doing here is simply looking ahead to see the potential pitfalls of situations before they arise and getting our plans in place. You eat good food for lunch when you have good food in the fridge already – in other words, create the conditions to make it as easy as possible.

3. Double up

There's something beautiful about creating positive habits that also eliminate negative ones at the same time. If you swap a chocolate bar for a nutriful snack, that's a double win. Skipping the work night in the pub and going to the gym instead will leave you feeling not 'just OK' tomorrow but breezy. Bringing lunch to work not only means you eat well but you also save money. Meditating before bed probably also eliminates some late-night phone scrolling. Rather than simply focusing on eliminating negatives, how about turning them into big fat positives instead?

4. Keystoning

A keystone habit is something you do to prompt another habit, which is harder to form. A great example of this would be a project management update meeting. It's easy, because of extrinsic motivation and accountability, to foresee everyone turning up and sitting in the room together at a set time every month for that meeting. No one wants to let the team down. But that meeting also acts as a kind of regular deadline and accountability 'check in' for the project, too, and creates a space where people come together and think about how well the project is going, anticipating the next bumps in the road. We don't create project meetings because we enjoy meetings, but because we know that habit becomes the trigger for the project's activities.

Similarly, when it comes to food, you might decide to work with a coach or accountability partner, to regularly 'check in' and talk about how you've been getting on. Or simply use an app or food journal to track your progress and what you're eating and cooking. These regular routines create the space for a little more mindfulness, as well the accountability (either towards ourselves or others) to stay on track.

5. Specificity
One of the most powerful and yet simple things you can do to boost your productivity is to get clear and specific. As Graham talks about in *How to be a Productivity Ninja*, defining the 'Next Physical Action' – being specific about how you plan to start – as well as creating a clear, measurable end point, will help to avoid procrastination. Simply saying 'I want to eat well' is not enough. Get specific with the habit you're trying to create (using questions like 'where', 'what' and 'how') and with the motivation (the 'why'). The clearer and more specific it is, the more chance you've got of identifying what will support or block it from happening.

6. Create the space
Creating the space is otherwise known as the 'President Obama suit technique'. Allow us to explain. Barack Obama was once asked why he only wore two kinds of suit: he basically had multiple versions of the same blue suit and multiple versions of the same grey suit. When asked why, he said, 'I'm trying to pare down decisions. I don't want to make too many decisions about what I'm eating or wearing – because I have too many other decisions to make.'

He understood the reality of decision fatigue and knew instinctively that as much as possible, he should try to create space in his life – through predictability and standard routines – so that as much of his attention as possible could be focused on the bigger issues. As we've discussed, changing these habits is harder if you're also trying to change everything else at the same time. So, take a step back and think about where this stuff fits. Choose your battles.

7. Get to know your lizard

This is another example of where great productivity advice applies just as easily to developing great food habits. The 'lizard brain' refers to our amygdala, part of the limbic system in our brain. It's the part of the brain responsible for survival mechanisms. The broken record of the lizard brain says: 'blend in, don't stand out'; 'avoid confrontation'; 'that's silly'; 'that's risky, don't do it', and so on. As such, the lizard brain doesn't like change, because change could be risky. It doesn't like innovation, because what if we're wrong? It doesn't even like success because that takes us out of our comfort zone.

So, the lizard brain will fill your mind with all sorts of silly stories of resistance, with the aim of sabotaging all your good intentions and ruining all your hard work. Unfortunately, the lizard brain and its resistance are a part of your brain that shouts extremely loudly. It needs to be heard, because it's part of our basic survival instincts, but if you let it get the better of your more rational and logical thinking, then you're stuck in procrastination, self-sabotage and feelings of guilt and fear. If you're regularly noticing your lizard brain, and being mindful of its irrational thought processes, you'll be much better placed to avoid its potential sabotage.

EXERCISE: DESIGNING YOUR NEW HABITS

Time:
10 minutes

What you'll need:
Pen and paper

Ninja mindset:
Mindfulness, Preparedness

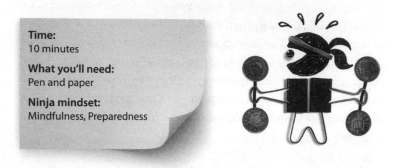

Tick three of the tactics here that you think are most likely to help you build a great new habit.

	✓
Cues and rewards	
If/then behaviour chains	
Double up	
Keystoning	
Specificity	
Create the space	
Get to know your lizard	

For each of the three you have ticked, what is the next physical action that you need to take to enable you to use it? (For example, if you're choosing 'create the space', then what choices are you going to eliminate, or what action will you take to create that space?)

KEEPING IT GOING – AVOIDING RESISTANCE

Many of the techniques and ideas we've discussed already in this chapter will help you to keep your lizard brain in check at the start of the process, but what happens when you find yourself at that perilous point, close to 'falling off the wagon'? Much of this is about creating momentum along the way, so that it feels like there's a positive and undeniable force sweeping you along to victory and doing everything you can to avoid sabotage – from your lizard brain or from other people.

CREATING AND MAINTAINING MOMENTUM

In looking at momentum, it's worth revisiting the issue of intrinsic and extrinsic motivation and thinking about how to create momentum that supports each of these. Here are two simple ideas:

Intrinsic motivation – the Seinfeld model

Jerry Seinfeld is one of the most successful comedians of all time. He was once asked the secret to his success. To be a better comic, you need to create better jokes. To create better jokes, you have to make sure you write every single day. His personal momentum technique was to put a red cross through each day on his large wall planner for every day that he wrote a joke: 'After a few days, you'll have a chain. Just keep at it and the chain will grow longer every day. You'll like seeing that chain, especially when you get a few weeks under your belt. Your only job next is to not break the chain. Don't break the chain.' In effect, the daily moment you add that red cross to the planner is a little signifier to the brain that you did your job today. You'll get the same effect using the Streaks app on your phone, as we mentioned earlier. It's important to

include a sense of ceremony here, even if the ceremony is only for one person.

Extrinsic Motivation – WhatsApp groups and the power of dopamine hits

One of the things we have both noticed when it comes to food is the power of sharing pictures of nutriful meals with others. Indeed, when Colette first coached Graham, we used WhatsApp chat as a way to share progress and updates. What's interesting is that the tiniest bit of feedback from this, such as someone else sending back a small comment like 'good job' or a 'high five' emoji, acts as its own little momentum-builder. The release of dopamine, our reward-chemical, makes us want to make the next meal as good, so that we get the same recognition. When we experimented with the Think Productive team, the same effect was true, and members of the team felt that strong sense of accountability and support simply by sharing their progress with others. There's powerful momentum to be gained simply from building a supportive community, whether it's a WhatsApp chat group, a Facebook group, or two people meeting face to face. In fact, we had some of our test readers for this book say that they ate healthier lunches before our feedback sessions, specifically so that they had a good food story to tell us on the call! Use the dopamine hits to drive your behaviour.

AVOIDING SABOTAGE

Sabotage can take many forms. It can be perpetrated by ourselves or by others. Here are a few ways to deal with it.

Self-sabotage

The lizard brain's chattering of resistance is the biggest cause of self-sabotage. Understanding the needs of the lizard brain – and then looking to outwit it – is important to keep things on track. The lizard brain looks for survival and predictability. What can you do that provides some of this, even in the changes you're making? For example, if you're used to a diet that reminds you of your mum's home cooking, and you're more partial to a pie than a salad, can you get some recipes for healthy, rainbow-filled pies or warm bakes? The lizard brain wants to feel that warm, fuzzy 'full stomach' feeling, and perhaps quinoa and salad alone isn't quite going to get you there.

The lizard brain will also tell you how pointless and stressful all of this change is: 'I've been doing this two whole days and I can't see any change in energy!' or 'This is too much effort, I don't have the time right now', or 'Other people are better at cooking than me. This isn't stuff that I can do.' The lizard brain wants you to quit quickly, so that it can scurry back into its cave of safety, security and predictability.

Make this safe for the lizard brain in whatever way you can. Tell your lizard this is just a temporary experiment and you'll be back to the pie and chips in a month (the lizard doesn't care that you're lying). Even just allowing for the possibility that the change isn't permanent will be enough for your lizard brain to calm down and give all the chatter a rest for a while.

Other people's sabotage

While you can exert a fair amount of control and pressure over your own lizard brain, sabotage comes from many places. Specifically, it may come from someone else's lizard brain! The day you bring healthy home-made snacks or a Tupperware box of salad into the office is a day where someone else may feel threatened or unsafe. They may feel jealous that you're trying something new. Jealous you made the effort and they didn't. And you'll hear about it.

'What's that rabbit food!', you'll hear. 'Those look like little turds.' And so on. The risk to you is that the more you fight against their lizard brain, the more they fight back. Try a little reverse psychology here. Instead of fighting back at all, let them have their rage. And when the moment is right: 'It's really simple to make, actually. Want to try some?' Suddenly their sabotage turns to curiosity, and you have the prospect of a new fuelie joining the ranks in the weeks ahead. Someone else to share the journey with.

Collect sabotage

If they're not quite coming around, then let's use some Ninja unorthodoxy and make this a game. Your goal is to collect as many 'acts of sabotage' as you can by the end of the week: 'Wish I had time for lunch' or 'Your food stinks' or 'I think I need your job with all this spare time to prepare food'. It builds your personal resilience, it shows that you are doing something different for the right reasons. Who wants to follow the pack anyhow?

Most importantly, it means you do not need to repeatedly defend yourself; this is wearing and tiring, and we do crack. Over time, if they don't convert, they get bored, we promise.

MAINSTREAMING HABITS

Finally, what are the other potential momentum-killers? Chances are, they fit into the category of 'other things you care about'. Perhaps your kids are not inclined to eat many vegetables, or your partner is set in their ways. You may need to employ some Ninja stealth and camouflage here to slip some veggies into the food you're preparing, even if it's slightly under the radar. We have it on good authority that if you chop a carrot finely enough, no one can tell it's there. Kefir, chia seeds, olive oil and nuts are all examples of things that can slip into bigger dishes pretty much unnoticed. What if you still need to cook two meals (one for you, one for the less fuelie members of the household)? What's going to use less energy here: converting them to the cause, or spending some time operating a two-meal routine? What feels palatable?

If you care about your gym routine, that's even more reason to get this right, but it's also more likely to leave you feeling hungry if you're burning a lot of energy in the gym, or leave you craving things like sugar more regularly. Again, think ahead and try to predict the scenarios this throws up. We'd recommend focusing on good portable snacks and making sure you're prepared with good food available in the first hour after a gym session (this is both where your body most craves nutrients and also where it makes best use of them restoratively).

Perhaps the thing you care about is a regular Wednesday night pub quiz, or, in Graham's case, a tragic hobby like travelling hundreds of miles to watch Aston Villa football games. In these instances, you need to be thinking about your Ninja preparedness many hours before you're stuck in front of a counter with only bad beige food to choose from.

As well as designing your habits, it's important to spend time playing out in your mind how these brilliant new habits sit alongside the other things that already fill your life. No life is

'Motivation is what gets you started. Habit is what keeps you going.'
– Jim Rohn

incompatible with making this stuff work. Everyone's weekly routine will have a few hurdles to jump over or some habit-breaking bullets to dodge. The point is to anticipate, plan and rehearse. You won't think of every scenario, but you'll ease the path to getting it right more often than not.

WHAT TO DO WHEN YOU FALL OFF THE WAGON

And finally, let's talk about the times you've done all that stuff and it still hasn't worked. Because none of us are perfect. A Productivity Ninja is a human being with great tools, the right mindset and brilliant habits, but that still doesn't make us a superhero. There are no special powers or guarantees that this stuff will always work. Our work would be really dull if that were true.

Think about it. Humans – with all our weirdness – make a damn good fist of changing habits and adapting, and doing this better every single day. We can delight others, inspire ourselves, and push the boundaries of what we thought was possible. But still we're human.

So, when you have a bad day, remember one of our key Work Fuel ingredients: 'consistency beats intensity'. In this circumstance, where you're feeling bad about yourself because you ate loads of sugary snacks and had chips in the pub, this is the best news. It doesn't really matter that much. Sure, it's suboptimal. Sure, that hang-over feeling in the morning won't be great. But consistency beats intensity. If you have a day full of non-Work Fuel, you've got a chain of great days behind you to look back and feel good about. Also: tomorrow.

Too much of the marketing around food and well-being and diet is based on guilt. Healthy food can sometimes become an unhealthy obsession. Practise some self-care. Give yourself credit where it's due. And use the days where it doesn't quite go right as the reminder that we're all human after all.

Imperfect. Fallible. Weird. And beautifully human.

Are you a Ninja?

▶ A Ninja uses self-awareness and mindful supervision of their 'lizard brain' to stay on track. Knowing the difference between whether something is an intrinsic or extrinsic motivator, for example, can be enough to alter course and help make a habit stick.

▶ A Ninja creates positive momentum and manages the sabotage, wherever it's coming from.

▶ When things don't go to plan, though, a Ninja knows that tomorrow is another day. Consistency matters more than intensity, and we're all humans, not superheroes.

EPILOGUE

GOOD NUTRITION CAN CHANGE THE WORLD

Whether you're a foodie or not, we hope you now consider yourself a fuelie. We hope you're convinced that putting the right fuel in your body is an important way to value your health, your well-being and your productivity. We believe that with this book, we can make work environments more positive and less stressful.

Perhaps a bit more creative first thing in the morning and certainly less tetchy in the afternoons. When Jamie Oliver showed that healthier, more balanced meals for school dinners made kids better learners in class, many schools revolutionized their mealtimes, banished the beige and started eating the rainbow. Of course, it's important that our children learn the right things, but the adults in our offices? They're in charge of stuff! They're running the world!

Our experience is that these simple steps can achieve powerful results. Indeed, working together a few years ago (Graham's coaching with Colette) was instrumental in Graham finding renewed energy, focus and productivity – and he was the 'Productivity Ninja' already, remember!

So, our mission in bringing you this book is that together we can change the world. One workplace at a time, one Productivity Ninja at a time, one meal at a time.

Breaking bread and sharing food is at the heart of a million human rituals, from Holy Communion to first dates, to team-building, to family dinners. Food is a sociable thing, and when you start to make some of the changes we've outlined in this book, we know you'll start to feel great and want to share your progress. When we were working together, we realized it was also important to share the struggles, voice difficulties, get help and just generally talk it through. As you embark on your journey towards better energy and Productivity Ninja status, have a think about who else you can recruit to our growing movement. A problem shared is a problem halved. Progress shared helps breed the motivation and momentum for tomorrow, too. This stuff just gets easier when you're not flying solo.

Of course, you can buy everyone you know a copy of this book. You'll also find downloadable resources and more information at **www.workfuel.ninja**. Please come through and say hi there too, and share your upgrades using the #workfuel hashtag. We'd love to hear your feedback and stories.

We know you'll have days when you're craving a Twix. And on some of those days, please just have a Twix. Because if you're focused on consistency instead of intensity, and getting it right most of the

time, then the odd treat is just fine. If you're remembering to eat the rainbow, ditching the beige, eating food made from plants instead of food made in plants and practising that all-important Ninja preparedness to make it all happen, then you'll be on the right track.

So take some action today, change another habit tomorrow, and fill your next weekly shop with a load more rainbow. Great energy and focus is just around the corner. Trust us, you'll forget what the 4 o'clock crash even was.

This book is designed for you to come back to as a reference, so we're guessing we'll see you back here very soon.

Until then, remember: you've got this.

Graham Allcott
Colette Heneghan

RECIPES

BREAKFAST

EGG TRAVEL MUFFIN

These are perfect for when you're on the go – hence the name. A great pre-prepared breakfast or lunch. You can serve them on their own or with a side salad, soup or baked sweet potato. They are tasty and filling.

12 servings
Time – 25 minutes

Ingredients:

Butter, for greasing

8 eggs

2 large pinches of sea salt

1 large pinch of black pepper

3 carrots or 3 courgettes, roughly grated (or a mix of both)

A handful of other veg – chopped red pepper, peas and spinach work well

1 onion (leek, spring onion and chives work too) – chop finely as these will not be precooked

1 large garlic clove, finely diced

Any spices or herbs, fresh or dried (e.g. dried oregano, cumin or fresh parsley)

A large handful of grated hard cheese, such as Cheddar, Jarlsberg or Parmesan (optional)

Equipment:

Muffin tray

Large bowl

Grater

Knife and chopping board

Method:

1. Preheat the oven to 200° C (400° F/Gas 6). Grease a muffin tray well with a little butter. Beat the eggs in a large bowl. Add the salt and pepper, all the grated and chopped vegetables or peas, the finely chopped onion and cheese, the garlic and any spices or herbs. Aim for 50% egg and 50% veg.

2. Pour the mixture into the prepared muffin tray, and bake for 12 minutes.

3. To check if they are done, give the muffin tray a shake – they should be set in the middle. If not, put them back in the oven for another 1–2 minutes.

4. Remove from the tray and leave to cool on a wire rack.

SAVOURY PORRIDGE

Serves 2
Time – 10 minutes

Ingredients:

6 tbsp porridge oats

2 tbsp chia seeds or ground flaxseed

1 carrot, peeled and shredded

360 ml (12½ fl oz) water

15 g (½ oz) stemmed and chopped kale or 30 g (1 oz) chopped spinach

2 tbsp nutritional yeast if you have it – it adds a cheesy taste and some vitamin B12 (it's good for energy)

½ avocado, chopped

2 tbsp roasted/raw pumpkin seeds

Smoked paprika

Salt and black pepper

Equipment:

Saucepan

Wooden spoon/spatula

Knife and chopping board

Method:

1. Combine the oats, chia seeds/flaxseed and carrot in a small saucepan over medium heat. Add the water. (Use more or less to achieve the consistency you prefer; 360 ml [12½ fl oz] will make a fairly thick porridge.)

2. Heat until simmering, then cook, stirring often, until everything is tender, about 5 minutes.

3. Stir in the kale/spinach and nutritional yeast.

4. Pour into a bowl and top with the avocado and pumpkin seeds. Sprinkle with smoked paprika. Season with salt and pepper to taste, and serve.

BREAKFAST BEANS

These can be eaten hot or cold, with an egg on top, with grated cheese or with a slice of toast.

Serves 2

Time – 25 minutes

Ingredients:

2 tins of any beans you like, such as cannellini, butter, kidney

1 tin chopped tomatoes

1 pepper, de-seeded and chopped

200 g (7 oz) mushrooms, chopped

1 handful of spinach

½ onion, chopped

Spices of your choice (we recommend oregano and garlic, turmeric and cumin, cayenne and cinnamon, or curry powder)

Olive oil

Salt and pepper

Equipment:

Knife and chopping board

Saucepan

Method:

1. Add the chopped onion, pepper and spices of your choice to a saucepan with a little olive oil. Stir until the vegetables are soft.

2. Add the rest of the ingredients and stir until it is all cooked through. This should take around 15 minutes, perhaps a little longer.

3. Season with salt and pepper to taste and serve.

LUNCH

FALAFEL

Makes 6 servings (12 falafels)
Time – 30 minutes

Ingredients:
2 tins of chickpeas
½ large red onion, roughly chopped
4 cloves garlic, roughly chopped
Handful of fresh parsley or coriander or both
2 tbsp olive oil and some extra to grease the baking sheet
2 tbsp lemon juice
2 tsp ground cumin or coriander (optional)
1½ tsp Himalayan rock salt
2 tsp baking powder

Equipment:
Food processor/blender
Baking sheet
Pastry brush (if you have one)
Spatula

Method:
1. Preheat the oven to 200° C (400° F/Gas 6). Brush or rub a baking sheet with a thin layer of olive oil.

2. Place the chickpeas, onion, garlic, parsley/coriander, olive oil, lemon juice, salt and spice/herb (if using) in a food processor.

3. Pulse the food processor 10 or 12 times, until the chickpeas are chopped and all the ingredients are mixed.

4. Sprinkle the baking powder over the mixture.

5. Continue to mix the chickpeas in pulses, scraping down the sides of the bowl as needed, until the mixture forms a ball when you squeeze it in your hand. (You can completely purée the mixture if you like a less chunky falafel.) If you are baking the falafels at a later date, pop the mixture in the fridge at this point (it will keep for up to 5 days).

6. Using your hands, scoop up some of the mixture and form it into a ball in your hand. The exact amount doesn't matter, just make sure that all your falafel balls are roughly the same size so they bake at the same rate.

7. Transfer the falafel balls to the baking sheet and gently press into patties roughly 2–3 cm (approx. 1 in) thick. Pressing the patties increases the surface contact with the baking sheet and makes the baked falafels crispier. If the patties break a little as you press them, just pat them back into shape.

8. Brush the tops with a little more olive oil.

9. Bake for 20–25 minutes, flipping the falafels halfway through. Be gentle when flipping them. If one does fall apart, just press it back together with the back of your spatula. When done, the falafel should be golden brown on both sides and feel dry to the touch, but still give a little when you press the middle.

10. Eat warm or at room temperature, or refrigerate for up to 5 days.

CREAMY GREEN POWER SOUP

A soup that personifies the Work Fuel advice 'eat your dark leafy greens'!

4–6 servings
Time – 15 minutes

Ingredients:

1 small onion, diced

1 large courgette, cut into 1 cm (½ inch)-thick slices

300 g (10½ oz) broccoli

300 g (10½ oz) chopped asparagus

150 g (5 oz) chopped kale or spinach

2 garlic cloves, minced

1 litre (1¾ pints) chicken stock or water with sea salt to taste

Equipment:

Lidded pot

Food processor/blender

Knife and chopping board

Method:

1. Put all the ingredients in a pot. Bring to the boil, cover and simmer until vegetables are fork tender and bright in colour, but not overcooked (about 5 minutes).

2. Remove from the heat and allow to cool. Purée the soup in batches in a food processor or using a hand blender. Serve in warmed bowls with a drizzle of olive oil.

Tip:

You could add a knob of butter or some coconut oil as you purée – the fat makes some of the vitamins in the veggies much easier for our bodies to absorb!

TOMATO & RED PEPPER SOUP

Serves 4

Time – 20 minutes

Ingredients:

1 tbsp olive oil

1 onion, finely chopped

2 sticks celery, finely chopped

2 large red peppers, de-seeded and chopped

4 cloves garlic, crushed

4 large tomatoes, chopped

1 400 g (14 fl oz) tin tomatoes

1 tin of cannellini beans

1 tsp chilli flakes (optional)

1 litre (1¾ pints) chicken/vegetable stock

Salt and pepper

Equipment:

Large saucepan

Food processor/blender

Knife and chopping board

Method:

1. Gently heat the olive oil in a large saucepan. Sauté the onion, celery, peppers and garlic for about 5 minutes.

2. Add the fresh tomatoes and cook for a further 3–4 minutes.

3. Add the tinned tomatoes, stock, cannellini beans and chilli (if using). Season well. Bring to the boil and allow to simmer gently for at least 15 minutes (leave for 30 minutes if you have the time).

4. Remove from the heat and allow to cool. Purée the soup in batches in a food processor or using a hand blender. Serve in warmed bowls with a drizzle of olive oil.

QUINOA, FETA & AVOCADO SALAD

Serves 2

Time – 25 minutes (15 minutes if quinoa is pre-cooked)

Ingredients:
80 g (3 oz) uncooked quinoa

16 cherry tomatoes, halved

2 sticks of celery, chopped

½ cucumber, diced

2 tbsp fresh coriander, chopped

½ red onion, diced

50 g (1¾ oz) feta cheese, crumbled

½ avocado, cut into chunks

Juice of 1 lemon

¼ tsp cayenne pepper or 1 tsp chilli flakes

Equipment:
Medium-sized pan

Bowl

Knife and chopping board

Method:
1. Pour enough boiling water to cover the quinoa in a pan and simmer for 15 minutes, adding more water if needed. Drain.

2. Mix everything together in a bowl and serve or refrigerate.

RATATOUILLE

This is such a versatile dish, and lends itself well to batch cooking. Accomplished chefs cook each ingredient separately and at different times to achieve the best consistency and taste. In the interest of nutrition and simplicity we just cook all together; you can use almost any veggies, so swap out ingredients for what you do have.

Serves 4
Time – 30 minutes

Ingredients:
2 medium peppers
1 medium aubergine
1 leek
10 mushrooms
2 onions
1 courgette
2 carrots
2 tins/jars/cartons of chopped tomatoes (400 g/14 fl oz each)
4 tbsp fresh basil or parsley, chopped
6 garlic cloves, crushed
1 tbsp paprika
Olive oil
Sea salt and black pepper

Equipment:
Large saucepan
Knife and chopping board

Method:
1. Chop all the vegetables into small chunks and add them to a large pan with a little olive oil. Cook for 5 minutes.
2. Add the rest of the ingredients and put a lid on the pot and simmer for 15 minutes.

DINNER

VEGGIE CHILLI

This is a quick chilli recipe using tinned ingredients, meaning less cooking and less chopping (you could also use jarred options). All the ingredients can be kept in the cupboard all the time as a back-up dinner, as they all have a long shelf life. Remember to check the labels on the beans: no added salt or sugar.

Serves 4
Time – 25 minutes

Ingredients:
1 tbsp coconut oil
1 onion, chopped
1 clove garlic, chopped
1 tsp chilli powder
1 tsp smoked paprika
1 tin kidney beans or mixed beans
1 tin chopped tomatoes
1 tin haricot beans, drained
1 tin adzuki beans, drained
Pinch of Himalayan rock salt

Equipment:
Saucepan
Spatula
Knife and chopping board

Method:
1. In a large saucepan, heat the oil, add the onion and garlic and fry for 5 minutes until soft and golden.

2. Add the chilli powder and smoked paprika and fry for a further minute.

3. Add the kidney beans in chilli sauce, the tomatoes, haricot beans, adzuki beans and salt, then stir thoroughly to combine.

4. Bring to the boil and then reduce to a simmer for 10 minutes. Stir occasionally.

5. Serve with yoghurt, chopped avocado, jalapenos and brown rice or make it a side dish for grilled chicken/fish/steak. Alternatively, serve with a baked sweet potato or even crumbled feta.

Tip:
At step 2 add in any extra chopped vegetables that you may have in the fridge: courgette, tomatoes, mushrooms, aubergine, spinach – whatever you like.

FISH CURRY

This is a super easy curry; most of the ingredients could come from the freezer and store cupboard. If you have the pre-chopped options in, it could be even quicker. The fish could be substituted for tofu to make a vegan version.

Serves 4
Time – 30 minutes

Ingredients:
1 tbsp coconut oil
1 chopped onion
2 tbsp medium curry powder
Thumb-sized piece of ginger, peeled and finely grated
4 garlic cloves, crushed
2 400 g (14 fl oz) cans chopped tomatoes
1 400 g can chickpeas

Salt and pepper

4 cod fillets (about 125–50 g/4½–5½ oz each – frozen or fresh)

1 lemon, zested and then cut into wedges

Handful of coriander, roughly chopped

Equipment:

Large frying pan

Knife and chopping board

Method:

1. Heat the oil in a large frying pan. Cook the onion over a high heat for a few minutes, then stir in the curry powder, ginger and garlic. Cook for another 1–2 minutes until fragrant, then stir in the tomatoes, chickpeas and some seasoning.

2. Cook for 8–10 minutes until thickened slightly, then top with the cod. Cover and cook for another 5–10 minutes until the fish is cooked through. Scatter over the lemon zest and coriander, then serve with the lemon wedges to squeeze over. Serve with a crunchy salad and brown rice or quinoa.

THAI SALMON FISHCAKES

Fishcakes are a great batch-cook option: double the quantities and freeze in twos. Swap the fish and potatoes for black beans for a vegan version.

Serves 4

Time – 30 minutes

Ingredients:

20 small new potatoes (with skins on)

4 salmon fillets

1 whole red chilli, de-seeded

1 tbsp fresh chopped coriander

1 thumb-sized piece of fresh ginger, peeled and finely chopped

8 cloves garlic, finely chopped

2 spring onions

1 egg, beaten

Juice of 1 lime

1 tsp coconut oil

A handful of wholewheat flour (for dusting)

Salt and pepper

For the dressing (alternatively, top with kimchi):

Juice of ½ lime

2 tsp mirin (sweet rice wine), or honey

4 tsp sesame oil

2 tsp soy sauce

Equipment:

Saucepan

Sieve

Tray or bowl

Frying pan

Knife and chopping board

Method:

1. Boil the potatoes in lightly salted water until tender. When cooked, drain and then mash roughly with a fork. Finely chop the red chilli, coriander, ginger, spring onions and garlic. Poach the salmon in boiling water for 7–10 mins. Allow to rest in a tray or bowl and then mix with the crushed potatoes, chilli, ginger, spring onions, garlic, coriander, lime juice and egg, and season.

2. Using wet hands, shape the mixture into 8 patties, dust in flour and gently pan fry in the coconut oil until golden.

3. Combine the ingredients for the dressing. Serve on a bed of leaves or steamed vegetables, with the dressing.

HEALTHY SNACK FOODS

CHOCOLATE POWER BITES

These chocolate and walnut bites taste amazing, are guaranteed to satisfy the biggest chocoholic and are packed with nutrition. Great as a quick breakfast addition or as a tactical snack for the office, commute or late-night working, ensuring you avoid the rubbish in the vending machine or at the station. They will keep in the fridge for a week or so, as well as the freezer for a month or so, making them a perfect snack to grab at the beginning of the day for later.

Makes 20 Bites
Time – 20 minutes

Ingredients:
100 g (3½ oz) walnuts
100 g (3½ oz) pitted dried dates
30 g (1 oz) raw cacao (or cocoa)
30 g (1 oz) chia seeds
60 g (2 oz) oats
3 tbsp coconut oil, more if needed
1 tsp vanilla extract
Optional brain boost – 1 tbsp reishi mushroom powder

Equipment:
Blender
Spatula
Storage container

Method:
1. Add all ingredients to the blender and pulse until well combined and finely blended. Use 3 tbsp coconut oil to begin with. If the

mixture is still crumbly and difficult to form into a ball after combining, use a little more.

2. Roll into small balls. Refrigerate for a firmer texture for an hour before serving.

Tip:
The quantities can be adjusted according to taste.

SPICY CUMIN HUMMUS

People think hummus is difficult to make, but in fact it's pretty easy, as well as being cheaper and far tastier than shop-bought varieties. You'll need a food processor but then it's simply a case of adding the ingredients and two minutes later you'll have a delicious, nutritious dip. Serving it with healthy vegetable crudités upgrades this to an even more nutritious level.

Makes a large bowl – equivalent to 2–3 supermarket tubs
Time – 5 minutes

Ingredients:
1 400 g (14 fl oz) can chickpeas
2 tbsp tahini (optional – it does make it taste amazing though!)
Juice of ½ lemon
1 clove garlic, finely chopped or crushed
½ tsp cumin powder
Salt and pepper
Variations to add before blending:
1 tsp smoked paprika (optional)
30 g (1 oz) flat-leaf parsley, finely chopped
2–3 pinches chilli flakes

Equipment:

Food processor

Spatula

Storage container

Knife and chopping board

Method:

1. Drain and rinse the chickpeas.

2. Combine the chickpeas, tahini, garlic, cumin, salt and half the lemon juice in a food processor and blend to a creamy consistency. Add water, a little at a time, until you reach the desired consistency.

3. Taste and season as required, adding more lemon or salt.

Tips:

► This hummus will keep for around a week in the fridge.

► Make a double batch and freeze half for a nutritious snack when you're pressed for time or have guests arriving.

KEFIR AND TAHINI DRESSING

Here's an example of how a quick and tasty dressing can be made, boosting the nutrition levels of your meal in minutes.

Serves 2

Time – 5 minutes

Ingredients:

1 tbsp tahini paste (or substitute with any nut butter)

1½ tbsp kefir (or substitute with yoghurt)

1 tsp lemon juice

1 small clove garlic

Pinch of salt

Equipment:

Blender (optional)

Method:

Add all ingredients to a blender and pulse until everything is combined. (Alternatively, finely chop the garlic, add to a bowl and stir together with the rest of the ingredients, until all combined.) Add a little water if a thinner consistency is desired. Eat immediately or store in the fridge for up to 3 days.

NOTES

Chapter 1

1. Andersen, T. G., Bollerslev, T. and Cai, J., 'Intraday and interday volatility in the Japanese stock market', *Journal of International Financial Markets, Institutions and Money*, 1999: https://pdfs.semanticscholar.org/83e6/04873c5e50cd5b617629bd7e5545029ae228.pdf

2. '"Healthy" foods have most of us confused, survey finds', CNN, 16 May 2017: https://edition.cnn.com/2017/05/16/health/healthy-foods-confusion-study/index.html
    'Health matters: obesity and the food environment', gov.uk: https://www.gov.uk/government/publications/health-matters-obesity-and-the-food-environment/

3. 'We spend more time watching food on TV than we do cooking it', *Telegraph*, 22 September 2016: https://www.telegraph.co.uk/food-and-drink/news/we-spend-more-time-watching-food-on-tv-than-we-do-cooking-it/

Chapter 2

1. Vinson, J. A. and Cai, Y., 'Nuts, especially walnuts, have both antioxidant quantity and efficacy and exhibit significant potential health benefits', *Food Funct.*, 2012, vol. 3, issue 134: http://pubs.rsc.org/en/content/articlehtml/2012/fo/c2fo10152a

2. Jeon, Sang Won et al., 'Inflammation-induced depression: Its pathophysiology and therapeutic implications', *Journal of Neuroimmunology*, 2016, vol. 313, 92–98: https://www.jni-journal.com/article/S0165-5728(17)30311-9/fulltext

3. 'Mediterranean Diet May Protect Against Alzheimer's Disease', Weill Cornell Medicine Newsroom, 4 May 2018: https://news.weill.cornell.edu/news/2018/05/mediterranean-diet-may-protect-against-alzheimer's-disease

4. Berti, V., Walters, M., Sterling, J., Quinn, C. G., Logue, M., Andrews, R., Matthews, D. C., Osorio, R. S., Alberto, P., Vallabhajosula, S., Isaacson, R. S., de Leon, M. J. and Mosconi, L., 'Mediterranean diet and 3-year Alzheimer brain biomarker changes in middle-aged adults', *Neurology*, 2018, 10.1212: http://n.neurology.org/content/early/2018/04/13/WNL.0000000000005527
    Mosconi, L., Walters, M., Sterling, J., et al., 'Lifestyle and vascular risk effects on MRI-based biomarkers of Alzheimer's disease: a cross-sectional study of middle-aged adults from the broader New York City area', *BMJ Open*, 2018, vol. 8, issue 3: https://bmjopen.bmj.com/content/8/3/e019362

5. 'Mediterranean Diet May Protect Against Alzheimer's Disease', Weill Cornell Medicine Newsroom, 4 May 2018: https://news.weill.cornell.edu/news/2018/05/mediterranean-diet-may-protect-against-alzheimer's-disease
    Mosconi, L. and McHugh, P. F., 'Let Food Be Thy Medicine: Diet, Nutrition, and Biomarkers' Risk of Alzheimer's Disease', *Current nutrition reports*, 2015, vol. 4, issue 2, 126–135: https://www.ncbi.nlm.nih.gov/pmc/articles/PMC4497956/

6. Whyte, A. R., Schafer, G. and Williams, C. M., 'Cognitive effects following acute wild blueberry supplementation in 7- to 10-year-old children', *Eur J Nutr*, 2016, vol. 55, issue 6: https://link.springer.com/article/10.1007%2Fs00394-015-1029-4

7. Kaur, H., Chauhan, S. and Sandhir, R., 'Protective Effect of Lycopene on Oxidative Stress and Cognitive Decline in Rotenone Induced Model of Parkinson's Disease', *Neurochem Res*, 2011, vol. 36, issue 8: https://www.ncbi.nlm.nih.gov/pubmed/21484267

8. Tarozzi, A., Angeloni, C., Malaguti, M., Morroni, F., Hrelia, S. and Hrelia, P., 'Sulforaphane as a Potential Protective Phytochemical against Neurodegenerative Diseases', *Oxidative Medicine and Cellular Longevity*, 2013, vol. 2013, Article ID 415078: https://www.hindawi.com/journals/omcl/2013/415078/

9. Dosz, E. B. and Jeffery, E. H., 'Modifying the Processing and Handling of Frozen Broccoli for Increased Sulforaphane Formation', *Journal of Food Science*, 2013, vol. 78, issue 9: https://www.ncbi.nlm.nih.gov/pubmed/23915112

10. 'Brain food: 6 snacks that are good for the mind', *Telegraph,* 23 Jan 2015: https://www.telegraph.co.uk/news/science/science-news/11364896/Brain-food-6-snacks-that-are-good-for-the-mind.html

11. Dash, P. K., Zhao J., Orsi, S. A., Zhang, M. and Moore, A. N., 'Sulforaphane improves cognitive function administered following traumatic brain injury', *Neuroscience letters*, 2009, vol. 460, issue 2, 103–107: https://www.ncbi.nlm.nih.gov/pmc/articles/PMC2700200/

12. Presley, T. D., Morgan, A. R., Bechtold, E., et al., 'Acute effect of a high nitrate diet on brain perfusion in older adults', *Nitric Oxide,* 2010, vol. 24, issue 1, 34–42: https://www.ncbi.nlm.nih.gov/pubmed/20951824

13. 'Can beetroot boost your brain and body?', bbc.co.uk: http://www.bbc.co.uk/programmes/articles/3cXzs0QnVVqvcvfWZ06C1BC/can-beetroot-boost-your-brain-and-body

14. Bovier, E. R., Renzi, L. M. and Hammond, B. R., 'A Double-Blind, Placebo-Controlled Study on the Effects of Lutein and Zeaxanthin on Neural Processing Speed and Efficiency', 2014, *PLoS ONE*, vol. 9, issue 9: http://journals.plos.org/plosone/article?id=10.1371/journal.pone.0108178

 Hammond, B. R., Miller, L. S., Bello, M. O., Lindbergh, C. A., Mewborn, C. and Renzi-Hammond, L. M., 'Effects of Lutein/Zeaxanthin Supplementation on the Cognitive Function of Community Dwelling Older Adults: A Randomized, Double-Masked, Placebo-Controlled Trial', *Front Aging Neurosci,* 2017, 9:254: https://www.ncbi.nlm.nih.gov/pmc/articles/PMC5540884/

15. Leidy, H. J. and Ortinau, L. C., 'Beneficial effects of a higher-protein breakfast on the appetitive, hormonal, and neural signals controlling energy intake regulation in overweight/obese, "breakfast-skipping," late-adolescent girls', *The American Journal of Clinical Nutrition*, 2013: https://academic.oup.com/ajcn/article/97/4/677/4576985

 Blom, W. A. M. and Lluch, A., 'Effect of a high-protein breakfast on the postprandial ghrelin response', *The American Journal of Clinical Nutrition*, 2006: https://doi.org/10.1093/ajcn/83.2.211

16. https://www.bluezones.com

17. Poly, C., Massaro, J. M., Seshadri, S., Wolf, P. A., Cho, E., Krall, E., Jacques, P. F. and Rhoda, A., 'The relation of dietary choline to cognitive performance and white-matter hyperintensity in the Framingham Offspring Cohort', *The American Journal of Clinical Nutrition*, 2011, vol. 94, issue 6, 1584–1591: https://academic.oup.com/ajcn/article/94/6/1584/4598197

18. Organic eggs have two times more omega-3s, seven times more beta carotene and three times more vitamin A than non-organic: Gray, J. and Griffin, B. A., 'Eggs: Establishing the nutritional benefits', *Nutrition Bulletin*, 2013, vol. 38, issue 4: https://onlinelibrary.wiley.com/doi/full/10.1111/nbu.12066

19. 'What does the blue MSC Label mean?': https://www.msc.org/what-we-are-doing/our-approach/what-does-the-blue-msc-label-mean

20. Benbrook, C. M., Butler, G., Latif, M. A., Leifert, C. and Davis, D. R., 'Organic production enhances milk nutritional quality by shifting fatty acid composition: a United States-wide, 18-month study', *PLoS One,* 2013; vol. 8, issue 12: https://www.ncbi.nlm.nih.gov/pmc/articles/PMC3857247/

21. Herrera, C., Smith, K., Atkinson, F., Ruell, P., Chow, C., O'Connor, H. and Brand-Miller, J., 'High-glycaemic index and -glycaemic load meals increase the availability of tryptophan in healthy volunteers', *British Journal of Nutrition*, 2011, vol. 105, issue 11, 1601–1606: https://www.ncbi.nlm.nih.gov/pubmed/21349213

22. Burton, P. and Lightowler, H. J., 'The impact of freezing and toasting on the glycaemic response of white bread', *European Journal of Clinical Nutrition*, 2017: https://www.researchgate.net/publication/51390869_The_impact_of_freezing_and_toasting_on_the_glycaemic_response_of_white_bread

23. 'Obesity rate triples', bbc.co.uk, 15 February 2001: http://news.bbc.co.uk/1/hi/health/1170787.stm

    'Statistics on Obesity, Physical Activity and Diet – England', 2018, digital.nhs.uk, 4 April 2018: https://digital.nhs.uk/data-and-information/publications/statistical/statistics-on-obesity-physical-activity-and-diet/statistics-on-obesity-physical-activity-and-diet-england-2018

24. Malhotra, A., Redberg, R. F. and Meier, P., 'Saturated fat does not clog the arteries: coronary heart disease is a chronic inflammatory condition, the risk of which can be effectively reduced from healthy lifestyle interventions', *Br J Sports Med,* 2017, 51:1111–1112: https://bjsm.bmj.com/content/51/15/1111

25. Chang, C. Y, Ke, D. S. and Chen J. Y. , 'Essential fatty acids and human brain', *Acta Neurol Taiwan*, 2009: https://www.ncbi.nlm.nih.gov/pubmed/20329590

26. Golomb, B. A. and Bui, A. K., 'A Fat to Forget: Trans Fat Consumption and Memory', *PLoS One,* 2015; vol. 10, issue 6: https://www.ncbi.nlm.nih.gov/pmc/articles/PMC4470692/

27. 'Trans fats, but not saturated fats, linked to greater risk of death and heart disease', *BMJ*, 12 August 2015: https://www.bmj.com/company/wp-content/uploads/2014/07/trans-fat.pdf

28. Martínez-Lapiscina, E. H., Clavero, P., Toledo, E., et al., 'Mediterranean diet improves cognition: the PREDIMED-NAVARRA randomised trial', *J Neurol Neurosurg Psychiatry*, 2013: https://www.naturalmedicinejournal.com/journal/2013-11/nuts-and-extra-virgin-olive-oil-improve-cognition-and-lower-risk-stroke

29. Simopoulos, A. P., 'The importance of the ratio of omega-6/omega-3 essential fatty acids', *Biomedicine & Pharmacotherapy*, 2002, vol. 56, issue 8: https://www.ncbi.nlm.nih.gov/pubmed/12442909

30. Ibid

    Simopoulos, A. P., 'An Increase in the Omega-6/Omega-3 Fatty Acid Ratio Increases the Risk for Obesity', *Nutrients*, 2016, vol. 8, issue 3, 128: https://www.ncbi.nlm.nih.gov/pmc/articles/PMC4808858/

31. Witte, A. V., Kerti, L., Hermannstädter, H. M., Fiebach, J. B., Schreiber, S. J., Schuchardt, J. P. , Hahn, A. and Flöel, A., 'Long-Chain Omega-3 Fatty Acids Improve Brain Function and Structure in Older Adults', *Cerebral Cortex*, 2014, vol. 24, issue 11, 3059–3068: https://www.ncbi.nlm.nih.gov/pubmed/23796946

32. Vinson, J. A. and Cai, Y., 'Nuts, especially walnuts, have both antioxidant quantity and efficacy and exhibit significant potential health benefits', *Food Funct.*, 2012, vol. 3, issue 134: http://pubs.rsc.org/en/content/articlehtml/2012/fo/c2fo10152a

33. Kratz, M., Baars, T. and Guyenet, S., 'The relationship between high-fat dairy consumption and obesity, cardiovascular, and metabolic disease', *Eur J Nutr,* 2013, 52: 1: https://link.springer.com/article/10.1007%2Fs00394-012-0418-1

34. Selhub, E. M., Logan, A. C. and Bested, A. C., 'Fermented foods, microbiota, and mental health: ancient practice meets nutritional psychiatry', *J Physiol Anthropol*, 2014, vol. 33, issue 1, 2: https://www.ncbi.nlm.nih.gov/pmc/articles/PMC3904694/

35. Lawrence, K. and Hyde, J., 'Microbiome restoration diet improves digestion, cognition

and physical and emotional wellbeing', *PLoS One*, 2017, vol. 12, issue 6: https://www.ncbi.nlm.nih.gov/pmc/articles/PMC5470704/

36. 'Fewer crops are feeding more people worldwide – and that's not good', *The Conversation*, 29 November 2017: http://theconversation.com/fewer-crops-are-feeding-more-people-worldwide-and-thats-not-good-86105

37. 'All you need to know about mainstreaming agrobiodiversity in sustainable food systems': https://www.bioversityinternational.org/fileadmin/user_upload/online_library/Mainstreaming_Agrobiodiversity/All_you_need_to_know_about_Mainstreaming_agrobiodiversity.pdf

38. McDonald, D. et al., 'American Gut: an Open Platform for Citizen Science Microbiome Research', *American Society for Microbiology Journals*, 2018: https://msystems.asm.org/content/3/3/e00031-18#sec-2

39. Ganio, M., Armstrong, L., Casa, D., McDermott, B., Lee, E., Yamamoto, L. and Lieberman, H., 'Mild dehydration impairs cognitive performance and mood of men', *British Journal of Nutrition*, 2011, vol. 106, issue 10, 1535–1543: https://www.cambridge.org/core/journals/british-journal-of-nutrition/article/mild-dehydration-impairs-cognitive-performance-and-mood-of-men/3388AB36B8DF73E844C9AD19271A75BF

40. Armstrong, L. E., Ganio, M. S., Casa, D. J., Lee, E. C., McDermott, B. P., Klau, J. F., Jimenez, L., Le Bellego, L., Chevillotte, E. and Lieberman, H. R., 'Mild Dehydration Affects Mood in Healthy Young Women', *The Journal of Nutrition*, 2012, vol. 142, issue 2, 382–388: https://academic.oup.com/jn/article/142/2/382/4743487

41. Manfo, F. P. T., Jubendradass, R., Nantia, E. A., Moundipa, P. F. and Mathur, P. P., 'Adverse Effects of Bisphenol A on Male Reproductive Function', in: Whitacre, D. (ed.) *Reviews of Environmental Contamination and Toxicology*, 2014, vol. 228, Springer, Cham: https://link.springer.com/chapter/10.1007/978-3-319-01619-1_3

    vom Saal, F. S., Akingbemi, B. T., Belcher, S. M., et al., 'Chapel Hill bisphenol A expert panel consensus statement: integration of mechanisms, effects in animals and potential to impact human health at current levels of exposure', *Reprod Toxicol*, 2007, vol. 24, issue 2, 131–138: https://www.ncbi.nlm.nih.gov/pmc/articles/PMC2967230/

42. 'Take back the tap: The big business hustle of bottled water': https://www.foodandwaterwatch.org/sites/default/files/rpt_1802_tbttbigwaterhustle-web.pdf

Chapter 3

1. Walsh, Bryan, 'Coffee and hormones: Here's how coffee really affects your health', precisionnutrition.com: https://www.precisionnutrition.com/coffee-and-hormones

2. Jung, S., Kim, M. H., Park, J. H., Jeong, Y. and Suk Ko, K., 'Cellular Antioxidant and Anti-Inflammatory Effects of Coffee Extracts with Different Roasting Levels', *Journal of Medicinal Food*, 2017: https://www.liebertpub.com/doi/10.1089/jmf.2017.3935

3. 'Warning issues over energy drinks', nhs.uk/news, 15 October 2014: https://www.nhs.uk/news/food-and-diet/warnings-issued-over-energy-drinks/

4. Zuñiga, L. Y., Aceves-de la Mora, M. C. A., González-Ortiz, M., Ramos-Núñez, J. L. and Martínez-Abundis, E., 'Effect of Chlorogenic Acid Administration on Glycemic Control, Insulin Secretion, and Insulin Sensitivity in Patients with Impaired Glucose Tolerance', *J Med Food*, 2018: https://www.ncbi.nlm.nih.gov/pubmed/29261010

    van Dijk, A. E., Olthof, M. R., Meeuse, J. C., Seebus, E., Heine, R. J. and van Dam, R. M., 'Acute Effects of Decaffeinated Coffee and the Major Coffee Components Chlorogenic Acid and Trigonelline on Glucose Tolerance', *Diabetes Care*, 2009: http://care.diabetesjournals.org/content/32/6/1023

5. Vicente, S. J. V., Queiroz, Y. S., Davidson Gotlieb, S. L. and Ferraz da Silva Torres, E. A., 'Stability of phenolic compounds and antioxidant capacity of regular and

decaffeinated coffees', *Brazilian Archives of Biology and Technology*, 2014, vol. 57, issue 1: http://www.scielo.br/scielo.php?pid=S1516-89132014000100016&script=sci_arttext

6. Zeisel, S. H., 'Choline: Needed for Normal Development of Memory', *Journal of the American College of Nutrition*, 2000, 19:sup5, 528S-531S: https://www.tandfonline.com/doi/abs/10.1080/07315724.2000.10718976

7. Reynolds, E. H., 'Folic acid, ageing, depression, and dementia', *BMJ*, 2002, vol. 324, issue 7352, 1512-1515: https://www.ncbi.nlm.nih.gov/pmc/articles/PMC1123448/

8. Visweswara Rao, P. and Gan, S., 'Cinnamon: A Multifaceted Medicinal Plant. Evidence-based complementary and alternative medicine', *eCAM*, 2014: https://www.research gate.net/publication/262229451_Cinnamon_A_Multifaceted_Medicinal_Plant

  Gary L. Wenk, *The Brain: What Everyone Needs to Know*, Oxford University Press: 2017

Chapter 4

1. Trougakos, J. P., Hideg, I., Hayden Cheng, B. and Beal, D. J., 'Lunch Breaks Unpacked: The Role Of Autonomy As A Moderator Of Recovery During Lunch', *The Academy of Management Journal*, 2014: https://www.researchgate.net/profile/Ivona_Hideg/publication/266967196_Lunch_Breaks_Unpacked_The_Role_of_Autonomy_as_a_Moderator_of_Recovery_during_Lunch/links/543fcb8d0cf21227a11b8098/Lunch-Breaks-Unpacked-The-Role-of-Autonomy-as-a-Moderator-of-Recovery-during-Lunch.pdf

2. Danziger, S., Levav, J. and Avnaim-Pesso, L., 'Extraneous factors in judicial decisions', *PNAS*, 2011: https://doi.org/10.1073/pnas.1018033108. Image redrawn with permission.

3. 'I think it's time we broke for lunch ...', *Economist,* 14 April 2011: https://www.economist.com/science-and-technology/2011/04/14/i-think-its-time-we-broke-for-lunch.

4. Conner, T. S., Brookie, K. L., Richardson, A. C. and Polak, M. A., 'On carrots and curiosity: Eating fruit and vegetables is associated with greater flourishing in daily life', *British Journal of Health Psychology,* 2015, vol. 20, issue 2: https://www.ncbi.nlm.nih.gov/pubmed/25080035

5. www.spicesforhealth.com: http://www.pwrnewmedia.com/2012/mccormick/science_alert_ginger/index.html

6. Lopresti, A. L., 'Salvia (Sage): A Review of its Potential Cognitive-Enhancing and Protective Effects', *Drugs R D*, 2016, vol. 17, issue 1, 53–64: https://www.ncbi.nlm.nih.gov/pmc/articles/PMC5318325/

7. Basagaaf, H., Tekkayab, C. and Acikela, F., 'Antioxidative and Free Radical Scavenging Properties of Rosemary Extract', *LWT – Food Science and Technology*, 1997, vol. 30, issue 1, 105–108: https://www.sciencedirect.com/science/article/pii/S0023643896901279

8. 'Wheeling Jesuit Researchers Present Findings on Scent-Behavior Link', wju.edu: http://www.wju.edu/about/adm_news_story.asp?iNewsID=1106&strBack=%2Fabout%2Fadm_news_archive.asp

9. Lejeune, M., Kovacs, E. and Westerterp-Plantenga, M., 'Effect of capsaicin on substrate oxidation and weight maintenance after modest body-weight loss in human subjects', *British Journal of Nutrition*, 2003, vol. 90, issue 3, 651–659: https://www.ncbi.nlm.nih.gov/pubmed/13129472

10. Belviranlı, M., Okudan, N., Atalık, K. E. N., et al., 'Curcumin improves spatial memory and decreases oxidative damage in aged female rats', *Biogerontology*, 2013, vol. 14, issue 187: https://link.springer.com/article/10.1007%2Fs10522-013-9422-y

  Shoba, G., Joy, D., Joseph, T., Majeed M., Rajendran, R. and Srinivas, P. S. S. R., 'Influence of Piperine on the Pharmacokinetics of Curcumin in Animals and Human Volunteers', *Planta Medica,* 1998, vol. 64, issue 4, 353–356: https://www.ncbi.nlm.nih.gov/pubmed/9619120

Chapter 5

1. Lowden, A., Moreno, C., Holmbäck, U., Lennernäs, M., et al., 'Eating and shift work – effects on habits, metabolism and performance', *Scand J Work Environ Health*, 2010, vol. 36, issue 2, 150–162: http://www.sjweh.fi/show_abstract. php?abstract_id=2898

2. 'Why you shouldn't eat late at night, according to science', *Telegraph*, 6 June 2017: https://www.telegraph.co.uk/health-fitness/body/shouldnt-eat-late-night-according-science/
   'Midnight Snacking is Bad for Your Brain', Smithsonian.com, 17 February 2015: https://www.smithsonianmag.com/science-nature/midnight-snacking-bad-your-brain-180954295/#pBfemCPFcp6rRXLe.99

3. Oike, H., Oishi, K. and Kobori, M., 'Nutrients, Clock Genes, and Chrononutrition', *Current Nutrition Reports*, 2014, vol. 3, issue 3, 204–212: https://link.springer.com/article/10.1007/s13668-014-0082-6

4. Lopez-Minguez, J., Saxena, R., Bandín, C., Scheer, F. A. and Garaulet, M., 'Late dinner impairs glucose tolerance in MTNR1B risk allele carriers: A randomized, cross-over study', *Clinical Nutrition*, 2018, vol. 37, issue 4, 1133–1140: https://www.ncbi.nlm.nih.gov/pubmed/28455106

5. Bandín, C., Scheer, F. A. J. L., Luque, A. J., Ávila-Gandía, V., Zamora, S., Madrid, J. A., Gómez-Abellán, P. and Garaulet, M., 'Meal timing affects glucose tolerance, substrate oxidation and circadian-related variables: A randomized, crossover trial', *International Journal of Obesity*, 2015, vol. 39, 828–833: https://www.ncbi.nlm.nih.gov/pubmed/25311083

6. Chaix, A., Zarrinpar, A., Miu, P. and Panda, S., 'Time-Restricted Feeding Is a Preventative and Therapeutic Intervention against Diverse Nutritional Challenges', *Cell Metabolism*, 2014, vol. 20, issue 6, 991–1005: https://www.cell.com/cell-metabolism/fulltext/S1550-4131(14)00498-7

7. 'Chew more to retain more energy', *Science Daily*, 15 July 2013: https://www.sciencedaily.com/releases/2013/07/130715134643.htm

8. Li, J., Zhang, N., Hu, L., Li, Z., Li, R., Li, C. and Wang, S., 'Improvement in chewing activity reduces energy intake in one meal and modulates plasma gut hormone concentrations in obese and lean young Chinese men', *The American Journal of Clinical Nutrition*, 2011, vol. 94, issue 3, 709–716: https://www.ncbi.nlm.nih.gov/pubmed/21775556

9. 'Japan gov't: Chew food 30 times', upi.com, 31 October 2009: https://www.upi.com/Japan-govt-Chew-food-30-times/47381257015651/

Chapter 6

1. 'Weight botchers: High-street food brands "breaching regulations" on nutrition labelling', *Sun*, 1 July 2018: https://www.thesun.co.uk/news/6671497/brands-under-valuing-carbs/

2. 'Cancer warning over processed foods that make up half of UK diet', *Telegraph*, 14 February 2018: https://www.telegraph.co.uk/news/2018/02/14/cancer-warning-processed-foods-make-half-uk-diet/

3. White, J. S., 'Straight talk about high-fructose corn syrup: what it is and what it ain't', *The American Journal of Clinical Nutrition*, 2008, vol. 88, issue 6, 1716S–1721S: https://academic.oup.com/ajcn/article/88/6/1716S/4617107

Chapter 7

1. de Castro, J. M., 'Eating Behavior: Lessons From the Real World of Humans', *Nutrition*, 2000, vol. 16, issue 10: https://www.ncbi.nlm.nih.gov/pubmed/11054584

2. 'Why you eat more when you're in company', bbc.com, 16 May 2018: http://www.bbc.com/future/story/20180430-why-you-eat-more-when-youre-in-company?ocid=twfut
3. Vartanian, L. R., Spanos, S., Herman, C. P and Polivy, J., 'Modeling of food intake: a meta-analytic review', *Social Influence*, 2015, vol. 10, issue 2: https://www.tandfonline.com/doi/full/10.1080/15534510.2015.1008037

Chapter 8
1. Taylor, R. S., Ashton, K. E., Moxham, T., Hooper, L. and Ebrahim, S., 'Reduced Dietary Salt for the Prevention of Cardiovascular Disease: A Meta-Analysis of Randomized Controlled Trials' (Cochrane Review), *American Journal of Hypertension*, 2011, vol. 24, issue 8, 843–853: https://www.ncbi.nlm.nih.gov/pubmed/21731062
2. Karami, A., Golieskardi, A., Choo, C. K., Larat, V., Galloway T. S. and Salamatinia, B., 'The presence of microplastics in commercial salts from different countries', *Scientific Reports*, 2017, vol. 7, article number: 46173: https://www.nature.com/articles/srep46173
3. '5 Reasons Why Salt is Good for You According to Medicine', DrStevenLin.com: https://www.drstevenlin.com/is-salt-healthy-5-reasons-to-eat-more-salt/
4. 'Is your daily social media usage higher than average?', *Telegraph*, 17 May 2015: https://www.telegraph.co.uk/finance/newsbysector/mediatechnologyand telecoms/11610959/Is-your-daily-social-media-usage-higher-than-average.html
5. 'Study finds clear differences between organic and non-organic products', Newcastle University Press Office, 16 February 2016: https://www.ncl.ac.uk/press/articles/archive/2016/02/organicandnon-organicmilkandmeat/
6. 'A study on the mineral depletion of the foods available to us as a nation over the period 1940 to 1991', *Mineral Resources International*: http://www.mineralresourcesint.co.uk/pdf/mineral_deplet.pdf

Chapter 9
1. 'Chopsticks: The cutlery conundrum', *Independent*, 31 August 2010: https://www.independent.co.uk/environment/chopsticks-the-cutlery-conundrum-2066109.html
2. 'Latest Weight-Loss Advice: Slow Down and Pay Attention', *Wall Street Journal*, 16 January 2007: https://www.wsj.com/articles/SB116891615189277255
3. 'Tips for boosting productivity with good office design', *Guardian*, 23 Jan 2014: https://www.theguardian.com/small-business-network/2014/jan/23/productivity-office-design
4. 'Exam revision students "should smell rosemary for memory"', bbc.co.uk, 4 May 2017: https://www.bbc.com/news/education-39780544
5. Shrivastava, A., 'A Review on Peppermint Oil', *Asian Journal of Pharmaceutical and Clinical Research*, 2009, vol. 2, issue 2, 27–33: https://www.researchgate.net/profile/Alankar_Shrivastava/publication/237842903_A_REVIEW_ON_PEPPERMINT_OIL/links/00b7d51be7ec239993000000.pdf
6. Moss, M., Cook, J., Wesnes, K. and Duckett, P., 'Aromas of rosemary and lavender essential oils differentially affect cognition and mood in healthy adults', *International Journal of Neuroscience*, 2003, vol. 113, issue 1, 15–38: https://www.ncbi.nlm.nih.gov/pubmed/12690999

   Cavanagh, H. M. A. and Wilkinson, J. M., 'Biological activities of Lavender essential oil', *Phytotherapy Research*, 2002, vol. 16, issue 4, 301–308: https://doi.org/10.1002/ptr.1103

   Diego, M. A., Jones, N. A., Field, T., Hernandez-reif, M., Schanberg, S., Kuhn, C., Galamaga, M., McAdam, V. and Galamaga, R., 'Aromatherapy Positively Affects Mood, EEG Patterns of Alertness and Math Computations', *International Journal of Neuroscience*, 1998, vol. 96, issues 3–4, 217–224: https://www.tandfonline.com/doi/abs/10.3109/00207459808986469#

7. 'Global Study Connects Levels Of Employee Productivity And Well Being To Office Design', prnewswire.com, 31 March 2015: https://www.prnewswire.com/news-releases/global-study-connects-levels-of-employee-productivity-and-well-being-to-office-design-300058034.html

   'Plants in offices increase happiness and productivity', *Guardian*, 1 September 2014: https://www.theguardian.com/money/2014/aug/31/plants-offices-workers-productive-minimalist-employees

8. 'Ashwagandha Benefits: Ease Stress and Anxiety by 44 Percent', universityhealthnews.com, 23 July 2018: https://universityhealthnews.com/daily/stress-anxiety/ashwagandha-benefits-ease-stress-and-anxiety-by-44-percent/

9. Stojanovska, L., Law, C., Lai, B., Chung, T., Nelson, K., Day, S., Apostolopulos, V. and Haines, C., 'Maca reduces blood pressure and depression, in a pilot study in postmenopausal women', *Climacteric*, 2015, vol. 18, issue 1, 69–78: https://www.ncbi.nlm.nih.gov/pubmed/24931003

10. Wachtel-Galor, S., Yuen, J., Buswell, J. A., et al. 'Ganoderma lucidum (Lingzhi or Reishi): A Medicinal Mushroom', in: Benzie, I. F. F., Wachtel-Galor, S. (eds.), *Herbal Medicine: Biomolecular and Clinical Aspects*, 2nd edition, 2011, Chapter 9: https://www.ncbi.nlm.nih.gov/books/NBK92757/

   Fatmawati, S., Shimizu, K. and Kondo, R., 'Ganoderol B: A potent α-glucosidase inhibitor isolated from the fruiting body of Ganoderma lucidum', *Phytomedicine*, 2011, vol. 18, issue 12, 1053–1055: https://www.ncbi.nlm.nih.gov/pubmed/21596546

Chapter 10

1. Li, Q., Kobayashi, M., Kumeda, S., Ochiai, T., Miura, T., Kagawa, T., Imai, M., Wang, Z., Otsuka, T. and Kawada, T., 'Effects of Forest Bathing on Cardiovascular and Metabolic Parameters in Middle-Aged Males', *Evidence-Based Complementary and Alternative Medicine*, 2016, 1: https://www.ncbi.nlm.nih.gov/pubmed/27493670

2. 'The Speedy Workout that Changes Your Brain', *The Cut*, 21 April 2017: https://www.thecut.com/2017/04/the-speedy-workout-that-changes-your-brain.html

3. Hogan, C. L., Mata, J. and Carstensen, L. L., 'Exercise Holds Immediate Benefits for Affect and Cognition in Younger and Older Adults', *Psychological Aging*, 2013, vol. 28, issue 2, 587–594: https://www.ncbi.nlm.nih.gov/pmc/articles/PMC3768113/#FN3

4. 'Tricking Your Brain to Avoid Jet Lag', psychologytoday.com, 2 January 2012: https://www.psychologytoday.com/gb/blog/prefrontal-nudity/201201/tricking-your-brain-avoid-jet-lag

5. 'Alcohol and Sugar', drinkaware.co.uk: https://www.drinkaware.co.uk/alcohol-facts/health-effects-of-alcohol/effects-on-the-body/alcohol-and-sugar/

FURTHER READING

NUTRITION:

Dr Lisa Mosconi (2018) *Brain Food: How to Eat Smart and Sharpen Your Mind*. London: Penguin Life.

Michael Pollan (2014) *Cooked: A Natural History of Transformation*. London: Penguin.

Dr Mark Hyman (2018) *Food: WTF Should I Eat?: The No-nonsense Guide to Achieving Optimal Weight and Lifelong Health*. London: Yellow Kite.

Max Lugavere (2018) *Genius Foods: Become Smarter, Happier, and More Productive While Protecting Your Brain for Life*. New York: Harper Wave.

Giulia Enders (2017) *Gut: The Inside Story of Our Body's Most Under-rated Organ*. London: Scribe.

Dr Michael Greger (2017) *How Not to Die: Discover the Foods Scientifically Proven to Prevent and Reverse Disease*. London: Pan Macmillan.

Dr Steven Lin (2018) *The Dental Diet: The Surprising Link Between Your Teeth, Real Food, and Life-Changing Natural Health*. London: Hay House.

COOKING:

Myles Hooper and Giles Humphries (2017) *Mindful Chef*. London: Century.

Jamie Oliver (2015) *Everyday Super Food*. London: Michael Joseph.

Jamie Oliver (2017) *5 Ingredients – Quick & Easy Food*. London: Michael Joseph.

Henry Firth and Ian Theasby (2018) *Bosh!: Simple Recipes. Amazing Food. All Plants*. London: HQ.

Miguel Barclay (2017) *Fast and Fresh: One Pound Meals*. London: Headline Home.

Dr Claire Bailey (2017) *The Clever Guts Diet Recipe Book*. London: Short Books.

HABITS:

Charles Duhigg (2013) *The Power of Habit: Why We Do What We Do, and How to Change*. New York: Random House Books.

ACKNOWLEDGEMENTS

GRAHAM AND COLETTE WOULD LIKE TO THANK:

The amazing team at Icon Books, especially Ellen Conlon for her patient editing and Philip Cotterell and Duncan Heath for their belief in this title and the series in general. Emma Brocklesby for creating brilliant illustrations with such care and love. Finally, our focus group participants, who all tested out the concepts and gave us feedback and the motivation to keep going, namely: Libby Barr, Julie Heneghan, Anna Litherland, Janet Kilpatrick, Darren Rogers, Jonathan Earle, Sean Slowley, Erin Buyers, Nicola Newton, Kathryn Sheridan, Sally-Anne Airey, Isabella Rushen, Zoe Williams, Hayley Watts, Grace Marshall, Matt Cowdroy, Matt Cooksey. Not forgetting our subject matter experts: Satu Jackson, May Simpkin, Lucinda Warner and Robert Tempelaar, who peer-reviewed and refined the science.

GRAHAM WOULD LIKE TO THANK:

The team at Think Productive; Colette for being such a huge inspiration over these last few years in making big changes to what I eat; Rob Geraghty without whom we'd have never met; friends too numerous to mention for indulging my conversations about black bean spaghetti, Mum for having Roscoe for a few days when I needed to get my head down.

COLETTE WOULD LIKE TO THANK:

Julie, my sister, for her support throughout the book journey and in all my other adventures too. Nicola for reading the very early versions over and over, being so supportive and positive. To Graham, for being such a brilliant, motivating and focused co-author (and the ultimate guinea pig for all things Work Fuel). My lovely Mum and Dad – June and Vincent. My cousin, Chantal, for her guidance and inspiration. And to all my close friends that have been there since the start of my new career, believing in me, giving constant support and tolerating my incessant chatter on all things nutrition related. Extra special thanks to Rodrigo, for encouraging and believing in me and helping to keep me well fuelled too – you make the best guacamole and gazpacho!

APPENDIX

THINK PRODUCTIVE

Graham's company, Think Productive, runs a range of practical productivity workshops, including:

- ▶ How to be a Productivity Ninja (full day implementation)
- ▶ The Way of the Productivity Ninja (short keynote session)
- ▶ Getting Your Inbox to Zero
- ▶ Fixing Meetings

Graham is also available for keynote talks.

Go to **www.thinkproductive.com**
for more details
or email **hello@thinkproductive.com**
to find out more.

OPTIMUM LIVING

Colette's company, Optimum Living, designs, manages and delivers health and well-being programmes globally. Workshop topics include: nutrition for energy, thriving leadership, understanding and managing stress, and the power of sleep.

Colette is also available for keynote talks.

For more details check out:
www.optimumliving.co.uk
or get in touch:
hello@optimumliving.co.uk

BRINGING **WORK FUEL** TO YOUR WORKPLACE ...

If you want to introduce the Work Fuel Way into your workplace, Graham and Colette bring all the fuelie goodness to life in their new venture:

- ► Online courses with Colette and Graham

- ► In-house company programmes run by Colette, Graham and their team of dedicated nutritionists

- ► Free checklists and printable resources

Find out more at:
www.workfuel.ninja

BEYOND BUSY
WITH GRAHAM ALLCOTT

Graham Allcott is your host for the **business podcast**
that asks the big questions. He explores the relationships
and tensions between productivity, work/life balance
and how humans define happiness and success. Through
in-depth interviews with founders, CEOs, sports-people
and professional clowns, you'll pick up tips and tricks,
inspiration and reading-list suggestions, as well as
spending time with interesting people in your ears.

Search 'Beyond Busy' in your podcast app
or go to **www.getbeyondbusy.com**
to get the latest episodes.

Colette is your host for **Work Fuel: The Podcast**, sharing honest and practical advice for a healthier, more balanced life. You will hear personal stories, ideas and tips from business professionals who are living proof of how to best take care of your well-being, no matter how challenging your work, social schedules or to-do lists are.

Tune in for tried and tested *Work Fuel* ideas that will improve your performance, resilience and energy.

Search 'Work Fuel' in your podcast app.

PUBLISHING SEPTEMBER 2019

BY GRAHAM ALLCOTT AND HAYLEY WATTS

FIXING MEETINGS

A PRODUCTIVITY NINJA GUIDE

MEET LESS OFTEN. FOCUS ON OUTCOMES. GET STUFF DONE.

How often do you find yourself sitting through meetings that should have been an email? Too much valuable time is wasted in meetings – it's time to think like a Ninja.

Productivity experts Graham Allcott and Hayley Watts want to start a meeting revolution, using practical advice to show you how to:

- Reduce the amount of time you spend in meetings
- Ensure that the meetings you do attend are great opportunities to get things done
- Influence others' meetings to be more action-orientated
- Have more time to focus on what matters

PUBLISHING SEPTEMBER 2019
ISBN: 9781785784750 (paperback)